A Year of Miracles

A Year of Miracles

Meditations Written By the Members of

Nicotine Anonymous

Huntington Beach, California

Nicotine Anonymous World Services
419 Main Street, PMB #370
Huntington Beach, CA 92648

Published by Nicotine Anonymous World Services,
a nonprofit tax-exempt corporation.

Nicotine Anonymous website address:
www.nicotine-anonymous.org

Printed in Canada
and printed on acid-free paper.

FIRST EDITION 2008

ISBN 0-9770115-4-2

978-0977011544

Preface

This book was written by Nicotine Anonymous members over many years.

Conference delegates decided to use members' own words, including some that may not be grammatically correct. Editors changed *smoking* to the generic *using nicotine* as much as possible. They eliminated references to brands or outside organizations by name. Editors also changed submissions to reflect each individual's experience instead of having meditations that talked about what *we do or should do*, or what *we experience.*

We have included Twelve Steps and Twelve Traditions after the meditations, and ended the book with a topical index. The final blank pages are for you to write your own meditation(s) and submit them for future publication.

Thank you for sharing your wisdom.

R elieve me of the bondage of self.
Help me abandon myself to the spirit.
Move me to do good in this world and show kindness.
Help me to overcome and avoid anger, resentment, jealousy and any other kind of negative thinking today.
Help me to help those who suffer.
Keep me alert with courage to face life and not withdraw from it, not to insulate myself from all pain whereby I insulate myself from love as well.
Free me from fantasy and fear. Inspire and direct my thinking today; let it be divorced from self-pity, dishonesty and self-seeking motives.
Show me the way of patience, tolerance, kindliness and love.
I pray for all of those to whom I've been unkind and ask that they are granted the same peace that I seek.

SEVENTH STEP PRAYER

My Higher Power, I place myself in your hands and humbly ask that my character defects be lifted from me so that I may help others. Please grant me willingness, courage, and strength so that through my actions I may reflect your love and wisdom.

God, direct my thinking in this upcoming day.
Humble me and guide me. Show me the way.
Keep dishonest and self-seeking motives away,
And do not allow self-pity to enter my day.

Keep selfish motives out of all my thoughts,
And remind me often of what you have taught.
When I am faced with some indecision today,
Show me the right course and guide the way.

Give me intuitive thoughts as you inspire me,
Or give me a decision so my mind can be free.
Teach me how to relax and take it easy too.
I know the right answers will come from you.

Don't let me struggle if the going gets rough.
Your same right answers will still be enough.
Place my thinking more on an inspired plane.
Let me come to rely on it and avoid the pain.

Above all, God, give me freedom from self-will.
Guide each step while I'm climbing the hill.
Remind me to ask for right action or thought
When I'm agitated, in doubt or even distraught.

Thy will be done. I'm no longer running the show.
I love you, God, and I just wanted You to know.

JANUARY 1

Every day we wake up,
we have choices to make up.
—A NICOTINE ANONYMOUS MEMBER

Each day I can begin by deciding my behavior regarding such things as hygiene, exercise, and food. I can choose to pray for guidance and support for this day. These choices will also affect my choice of attitude with which I begin my day. I can create a plan with these choices, and then take active steps to carry it out as well as I can at each moment. I seek "progress, not perfection." I humbly practice the intentions of my own choices.

As a nicotine addict, once I choose to use my drug of choice, I begin to lose the gift of choice. Using controls my behavior and attitudes. Using controls who I associate with, the places I go, and the situations I end up in. Using causes me to lose choices all along the way and thus become lost. Eventually I may get sick, institutionalized, or die as a direct result of this addiction.

Choosing a path of recovery, rather than the closed cycle of addiction, improves my life. Recovery opens new possibilities beyond my wildest dreams or in ways that I had previously been too sick to see.

Today, I am aware of my power to make new choices, create new behaviors, and enjoy new attitudes that improve the quality of my life.

I came to meetings for three years and still
couldn't stop, until I finally realized it was true,
I couldn't stop.
— NICOTINE ANONYMOUS:THE BOOK

I was coughing so hard I was afraid I was going to pass out. I did not want to eat because I always went into a coughing fit afterwards. I was sleeping in my chair instead of in my bed because I could not breathe lying down. I cleared my throat constantly. I had bronchitis twice in the past three months. I had lost so much weight I could see the veins in my stomach. I knew I had to quit, but how many times had I said that before but kept on smoking?

Then it dawned on me. I really was powerless so God was going to have to do it, or it would not get done. Instead of fighting the compulsion, my part became giving it to God. I "turned it over" every time the urge came. They said God could and would if He were sought. They were right. I cannot remember the last time I had the urge to smoke, and it has been eight months.

*Today, I thank God for doing for me
what I cannot do myself.*

I no longer count the value of a day by feeling the
change in my pocket, but by feeling the change in
my heart.

—NICOTINE ANONYMOUS MEMBER

When I was a child, much of how good I felt depended on what I got: whether attentive care, birthday presents, or just getting my way, the focus was on getting something from the outside world. I continually counted my marbles and felt either powerful and satisfied, or resentful when I compared my pile to others'.

Like many others, I became addicted when I was still a child, starting with nicotine. I wanted to get away with or get more, but found I could never get enough.

In recovery I learned about the tool of service and carrying the message by practicing the Program's principles, such as humility, kindliness, and patience "in all our affairs." Maturity came when I realized my real value comes from what I have to offer and freely give it away.

*Today, I will count my blessings and
offer them to others, knowing this is
the source of true wealth.*

Doing the best at this moment puts you in the best
place for the next moment.

—OPRAH WINFREY

I was possessed by a demon of indescribable power, a demon that
seemed oblivious to my will, a demon that robbed my sense of
self-worth. I could list dozens of reasons, but really needed no
provocation to continue to pamper my addiction. I could set no
boundaries for my need to smoke. Why else would I light another when
I had one burning?

I found relief through surrender. Divine intervention coupled with
my sincere desire to quit provided the dynamic strength to break free
from this demon.

There were many obstacles on my path to ultimate cessation. My
un-medicated anger made me a menace to those around me and to
myself. But my desire to quit and stay quit was stronger than the anguish
over my inability to control my emotions.

I am nicotine-free. Recovery allowed me to make amends for my
aggressive and self-absorbed behavior. Living nicotine-free is itself a
living amend.

*Today, I thank God I have the ability
to deal with the inevitable conflicts in
life, without using nicotine.*

Admitted we were powerless over nicotine.
—STEP ONE

I tried to stop using nicotine every day for at least twenty years. It never occurred to me that I was addicted to nicotine. It never occurred to me that I was powerless over something. I had a million and one excuses about why I was still puffing away: My life was too stressful, someone upset me, I had a test, a deadline, a cold, etc. It was quite amazing the number of different problems that kept me from quitting. It seemed much more acceptable to me to have a reason why it was impossible to quit right now than to think I had absolutely no control over my stopping.

My friends and colleagues listened to my many schemes to defeat nicotine. After a week or two they would see me using as much as usual. After a while, I grew too embarrassed to tell people that I was quitting.

When I first came to Nicotine Anonymous I was just going through the motions of the latest scheme that I had discovered. At some point I thought that I could just go to the meetings and hope that whatever knowledge the group had would seep into my brain. I was powerless and at last I understood Step One.

*Today, I understand I had been participating
in a grand hoax, I haven't given up
anything at all.*

In order to succeed, your desire for success should
be greater than your fear of failure.
—BILL COSBY

It almost seemed like I had to get blinded by the addiction's full force
of power before I could see the light. I stumbled around for years,
making half-hearted attempts at quitting. Sometimes it got me out
into the light temporarily. Maybe I was able to stop while waiting for a
medical diagnosis to come back, or when I got disgusted with myself
while listening to a child's pleading. Whatever the reason, it never
worked for long because I secretly believed I could never stay quit. I
thought I had to quit forever, not "just for today."

Then I found Nicotine Anonymous and learned to trust that if other
people could do it, people who were as hooked as I was, maybe there
really was hope for me. It became just a matter of time before the
freedom came as well.

*Today, I will bask in the light I have
found this side of addiction.*

Seek the help you need.

—MY SPONSOR

When I got to recovery after years of chemical abuse, I needed so much help to get well. I am still not totally well. I was beaten up so badly I started with a treatment group and was directed to other Twelve Step Programs.

The final drug to quit was nicotine, perhaps for me the hardest. I was so filled with denial that it was a serious problem. I also felt I could not quit or get a moment's peace without nicotine. I was drawn to Nicotine Anonymous and you helped me quit tobacco.

Previously I had problems with working. Now I own my own business.

I thank God for the willingness to seek help for problems, for the willingness to live in the solution, and for revealing new hope and truth.

Today, I pray for willingness and serenity.

Create the kind of self you will be
happy to live with all your life.
—FOSTER C. MCCLELLAN

When I was smoking I was selfish and self-centered. I was obsessed with me. I would avoid people, places and things that interfered with smoking. No movie theaters, no long car rides, no parties with non-smokers.

When I woke up in the morning, the first thing I did was to light up in bed. The last thing I would do is smoke in bed before turning out the light. How I resented people and places where I could not smoke.

Today I am free. I do not want or need to smoke, and I do not worry about where and when I can smoke. I am not as self-centered as I was.

Thank you, God, and our Twelve Steps. I am more willing to think of other people and their needs. I am more likely to reach out and call for help, and to offer help to others.

---

*Today, I am comfortable and free to choose
my companions and locations.*

No one can make you feel inferior
without your consent.
—ELEANOR ROOSEVELT

What can be more demeaning than being a "dumpster smoker?" You know what I mean. I'd leave my job to go outside and smoke; or, leave the theatre, or the restaurant, or my own home. I felt so humiliated. I knew I needed that smoke no matter the cost, time or place. No matter who was hurt, or offended, or annoyed, nicotine was my be-all and end-all. I couldn't live with it, and I couldn't live without it.

No wonder I had no self-worth. Caught, trapped, snared, and hopeless. Finally, I was desperate enough to go to a Nicotine Anonymous meeting. I was fearful. Would they accept someone who was still smoking? Or throw me out?

Thank You, Higher Power, for giving me a place to grow with other nicotine addicts who understand. Thank You for the tools of the Program, meetings, slogans, sponsorship, and, especially, prayer. By Your grace, I am free for today, and becoming more whole and complete each day.

*Today, I choose to use the tools of the
Program to continue growing.*

No need to say we're sorry,
No need to make amends,
We're through with being lovers,
And we never have been friends.

—NICOTINE ANONYMOUS MEMBER

The relationship I had with tobacco was like a dysfunctional, yet seductive, love affair. Even though I was warned to stay away, I was intrigued all the more. I wanted to have whatever I was not getting in my life. I felt a need that came from my longings and my let-downs.

I grew up with an influence to smoke, literally all around me. Advertising and movies still portray those involved with tobacco as possessing power and passion. As a youngster I lost my virginity coughing awkwardly, but I soon learned how to hold my lovers and kiss them. I clutched them wherever I went.

Listening at meetings I hear the truth, tobacco was not really a faithful friend. It was a bully always wanting its way. It did not care at what cost or what I lost. When I finally kicked them, there was no need to apologize.

*Today, I choose to create relationships based
on trust and care, not deceit and danger.*

We cannot change anything unless we accept it.
Condemnation does not liberate, it oppresses.
—C. G. JUNG

All the curses I can utter, all the self-loathing I can swallow, will not bring about long-lasting change. These patterns of behavior only reinforce the negative cycle of addiction. I used nicotine to numb my negative feelings. Condemnation just triggers me into my addiction.

Step One asks me to accept and admit that I am a powerless addict and that my life is suffering from the continual abuse of nicotine. Until I accept the truth of my circumstances I am merely pretending, rather than tending to my life. Only as I move toward the complete acceptance of myself can I be truly open for the healing I receive from my Higher Power.

Until then, I repeat the same old excuses and defects over and over again while expecting different results. This insanity always takes me to the same place. I put nicotine into my body for relief, but then I feel condemned and demoralized afterwards.

With acceptance I can stop running away. The trigger to condemn myself is defused. In recovery I surrender to the truth and the help that can set me free.

Today, I accept the truth. My surrender eases
the harshness and opens me to real change.

The attempt to develop a sense of humor and to see
things in a humorous light is some kind of a trick
learned while mastering the art of living.

—VICTOR E. FRANKL

As I think back to the beginning of my nicotine-free days, I felt so depressed. I felt like I could cry at any moment. There were actually times when I did cry. I thought that I had lost my best friend. I did not think I would ever be happy again.

As time went by, I realized that I was going to survive; not only survive, but actually live a happier life. I learned most of this from my Nicotine Anonymous friends. I remember at one meeting, I was saying how difficult it was to pass my old nicotine supply shop without being tempted to go inside. One of the ladies said, "The way I got over that was to wave at the store as I drove by, and remind myself that I don't need them anymore."

The next time I drove by, I tried her idea, and it not only worked, it made me laugh. I realized that I had not laughed much at the beginning, and I think that was one of my turning points. I started seeing humor in more and more areas of my life. I was starting to enjoy again. Whenever I saw someone standing at the back door of their place of employment, next to the dumpster, I would feel a great sense of relief that I did not have to do that anymore. All the things that I formerly missed were not bothering me anymore because I changed my attitude. I decided to start to enjoy my new life, and my new choice.

Now, I laugh easily. I look for ways to enjoy my new life. And, I still wave at the nicotine supply shop every once in a while.

Today, I will laugh as often as I can; it
is like jogging for the inner organs.

The creation of a thousand forests is in one acorn.
—RALPH WALDO EMERSON

How I got from one moment to the next was a series of miracles, a collective effort of phone calls and emails to Nicotine Anonymous friends, a goodbye ritual to the poison stuff. I was met with humor and compassion. A few moments, hours, days at a time, was all I could muster. Anything bigger was way too scary.

When I got to the next meeting, I was thrilled to be one of them and free. I think I laughed, I mean really laughed hard during those first few weeks, more than I ever had in my life. I probably laughed over the fact that I could not believe I was not smoking and relying on the substance I had depended on for the last twenty years. I guess my willingness was the first miracle. It paves the way for more, and I am ever grateful.

Today, I will remember miracles come
if I am willing to accept them.

It is better to light one candle
than to curse the darkness.

—CHINESE PROVERB

When my "nicodemon" is telling me, "life sucks, so grab nicotine," I have a choice whether to keep that belief or change it. Sometimes life sucks. That is life. But, it might be unpleasant whether I smoke or not. For me the best way to handle that feeling is to acknowledge it and ride it out, like a wave or an urge to use, and to decide on a new belief.

When life dishes out discomfort and pain, I can ask myself, "Is this life or death? Can I use some humor in the here and now of it all? Is there a way out?" Usually there is a better way.

Today, I will love myself regardless of
what life brings. Nothing is absolute.

I have a dream . . .
— DR. MARTIN LUTHER KING, JR.

To take the First Step and admit that I had been living a nightmare also provided me with an opportunity to admit, "I have a dream." When I turn the light of my attention and intention on a subject, I illuminate my desire. When I as a person in a nicotine nightmare join hands with others who are working toward the dream to be clean, a greater Power becomes available to me.

I had the dream to be clean for years. I had set quit dates on certain holidays and on my birthday. Over and over my dream was dashed on the rocks of my addiction. I could not accept the craving for nicotine long enough, so I kept re-infecting myself with another dose. My addiction deflated my dreams, soured my hopes, and leaked cynicism into celebrations.

Becoming part of this Fellowship breathed new life into my dream. I witness real joy as others celebrate their nicotine-free anniversaries.

Happy Birthday Martin. Thank you for the courageous passion of your dream. Although oppressors come in various forms, through Fellowship, people can work together to be "free at last." Yes, I too, have a dream to live free and clear.

*Today, I will celebrate
my dreams and freedom.*

When we fear our continued addiction more than
we fear being without it, our recovery will begin.
—NICOTINE ANONYMOUS MEMBER

After smoking for twenty-plus years, I imagined that I could recover immediately. I leaned that quitting is only the first small step in the process of recovery. In taking the Steps, I realized that my recovery required a complete overhaul of my personality, emotions, motivations, needs, character strengths and defects. I had to learn to deal with feelings, good and bad. After years of recovery, I can laugh, I can cry, I can finally feel without being afraid or trying to cover up my feelings with a drug. The Steps taught me a new way to be, they taught me to be free.

I actually feared being without my cigarettes more than I feared death itself. Nicotine Anonymous gave me a glimmer of hope that I could survive nicotine-free. The Program gave me tools to deal with withdrawal and cravings, my emotions, and life's crazy ups and downs. I feel as if I have been reborn. I no longer crave nicotine; I have experienced a genuine metamorphosis.

Early in my recovery process I began to understand that I wasn't weak, or stupid, or damaged goods; I was simply addicted to an extremely powerful drug. The pain of withdrawal is brief but the pain of continued addiction was devastating to my body mind and spirit. Withdrawal was a mere pinprick compared to the pain and suffering of remaining addicted. I learned to depend upon support and encouragement instead of nicotine to help me cope. The Program led me to a higher level of being, a place where I find truth, serenity, love, compassion and most of all, hope for a happy and healthy future.

*Today, I know that recovery is evolutionary, Recovery requires
patience, dedication and a willingness to be free of addiction.*

Develop success from failures.
Discouragement and failure are two of the
surest stepping stones to success.
—DALE CARNEGIE

I lost a dear companion to lung cancer on his fifty-eighth birthday. He smoked about three packs of non-filtered cigarettes every day. The following year, many others I was closely connected with were also victims of heart disease, strokes, emphysema, and other nicotine related deaths. I was getting a message but was unable to quit.

Once I quit for five and a half months on my own. But, I was unable to deal with daily upsets and finally gave in to anger. One day, I smoked two packs of cigarettes in a few hours after an argument with my manager over something silly. I tried for thirteen years to quit, but could not do it.

I found out about Nicotine Anonymous meetings from a lady who was not using nicotine and who was not crazy. Even though I was still using nicotine, I went to a meeting. Three months later God helped me quit. It was tough, but with God I can do it.

Today, I will remember to surrender every difficulty to my Higher Power. I no longer have to rely on myself or any drug to deal with life's upsets.

Of course there is no formula for success
except perhaps an unconditional acceptance
of life and what it brings.
—ARTHUR RUBENSTEIN

Tobacco poisoned my body. It gave me bronchitis and coughing fits, and prompted lectures from doctors and friends. It poisoned my self-respect and my relationships with other people. Nicotine addiction poisoned my love for myself. I thought I could not give it up.

Every time I quit using nicotine I felt pain. I would go back to tobacco to not feel the pain.

What I learned in Nicotine Anonymous is that I need to feel the pain, surrender, and accept the pain of quitting tobacco and start loving life. The pain passes and good feelings take its place. I still feel the pain of living at times. That is part of life. But, thank You God, I am no longer poisoning myself and my relationships.

Going through the pain of living life free of tobacco is well worth the smober life I have enjoyed over these years.

*Today, I recognize that growth is sometimes
painful. I welcome the growth.*

He that will believe only what he can fully comprehend
must have a very long head or a very short creed.

— C.C. COLTON

In this Program of recovery I heard that miracles happen. As a
newcomer, I was skeptical of the idea. Like other nicotine addicts I
needed a long time before I was ready to admit I needed the help of a
recovery program. I had become accustomed to an instant solution I
could hold in my hands. The notion of accepting a reality I could not
grasp was beyond me, at first.

The more time I spend clean, the clearer I see the world around me.
With the veil of nicotine gone I can witness more of Nature's beauty. I
smell it, taste it, and touch it. I can now celebrate the creation. I am no
longer trying to hide from this marvel called life. My first miracle may be
that I stopped using nicotine, but this was only the beginning of my
amazement.

Today, I am learning to embrace miracles.

> But is a fence over which few leap.
>
> — GERMAN PROVERB

Taking a moment to consider all the big and little things I have thought about doing during my life, but.... How many times have I put a but in my way and turned aside? How many times have I put a butt in my mouths and turned aside? And how many times have I felt like an ass or a butt because I turned and missed an opportunity?

Okay, let me take a good breath, this Program is not about feeling more shame. Like many others I have been trying too long to numb myself from that. However, my buts list could be added to my Fourth Step inventory. The more I see where I turned away, the more I see where I need to head.

I want to live my life without any more ifs, ands, or buts ... or butts.

Today, I pray, may my detours be lifted so that I can move more freely towards my desires.

JANUARY 21

Unhappy is the man, though he rule the world,
who does not consider himself supremely blest.
—LUCIUS ANNAEUS SENECA

How easy it is to forget all that I have to be grateful for. If a sunrise and sunset were a once-a-year occurrence, it would be a national holiday. Businesses and schools would be closed, and everyone would plan to be with the people they love, in the place they love.

No doubt about it, it would be a grand day for celebration.

How often do I remember to be grateful? I am grateful that my nicotine addiction is no longer active. I am grateful I am no longer driven to buy and use that drug. It's so easy when I'm annoyed, or disappointed, or "hungry-angry-lonely-tired" (HALT), to forget that I'm free of nicotine for today and very grateful to my Higher Power for this Program and the people in it.

If I forget to be grateful, Higher Power, give me a little nudge—a beautiful sunrise, sunset, a glorious day, a call from a friend, an enthusiastic hello from my pet, an empty pack of cigarettes on the ground that isn't mine.

Today, I pause to be grateful. I know that an
"attitude of gratitude" will keep me free.

What will I do today? It may depend upon which
"will" I chose to listen to.

—NICOTINE ANONYMOUS MEMBER

Human beings have what we call free will. This may be true, but the people, places, and things in our surroundings also influence our thinking. We say we have willpower, but even normal people find themselves admitting, "I knew I shouldn't have done that, but...."

As an addict my willpower has not been sufficient to help me stop using drugs. After all, my will has been conditioned with the determined thinking of: I want nicotine, my drug of choice; I will have nicotine, my drug of choice.

"Coming to believe that a Power greater than myself can restore me to sanity" can mean becoming open-minded to consider the guidance and wisdom of a counselor and/or a sponsor, the group, the Program, and a belief in a Higher Power of our own understanding.

Today, as I open myself to the possibility of being restored, I do not lose my will; I gain a greater Will to help recover my life.

> No one is as capable of gratitude as one who has
> emerged from the kingdom of night.
> —ELIE WIESEL

I have a plan for today. Having this plan will reduce anxiety and confusion in my day. This will not be an unusual day for me, as far as I know now. Maybe I will not get everything done that I would like to do today, but there is one big project I will chip away at. Like eating a whale, piece-by-piece I will get it done.

I find many surprises each day. Many of them are the silly things, or beautiful joys that I do not know how to plan. All in all, it is just another ordinary day. Still, to me it will be special.

Today, for twenty-four hours, I will not smoke. Deep inside, that makes me feel very, very good. Today my fingers will not be yellow and smell, because I will wash and use creams to help heal the skin. I forgive myself freely for that and every other harm I caused myself by smoking. I was doing the best I knew how at the time. But today I am free. My body is repairing itself in wonderful ways. And I am healing myself emotionally and spiritually as I continue to work the Program. I use my common sense and apply the things that make good sense to me. That is hard but satisfying work.

I am free. I am stronger than the terrible curse of nicotine addiction.

Today, I feel very special and good. I am free
from nicotine and free to live life fully.

I can use nicotine if I want to, but for this very
moment, I choose not to.
—NICOTINE ANONYMOUS MEMBER

Because one of my reasons for using nicotine was to help me relax, little did I know. Since I quit fueling my addiction, I have been helped tremendously by finding new and healthier means of relaxation. A few of my favorites are bicycling, stretching, taking a yoga class, creating arts and crafts, and meditating.

Now that I am on the road to recovery, I am rediscovering what I like doing and what brings me peace. Perhaps my favorite stress reliever of all is my monthly massage. When compared to the money I used to spend on nicotine, a massage once a month sure feels like a "softer, easier way."

Today, I acknowledge the depths of the pain and despair that nicotine brought me, and although it may feel scary, "just for today" I choose not to use any form of nicotine.

He who is being carried does not
realize how far the town is.

—NIGERIAN PROVERB

During my years of active nicotine addiction, I did not know the many experiences and the thousands of feelings I was blunting by staying drugged. Because it was legal and it was socially acceptable at the time, I had no awareness that I was zoning out, literally being carried through life without facing my emotions.

Today I no longer live behind that nicotine fog. Today I am free to feel, and to experience all that life has to offer. "Living life on life's terms" is not easy and I have needed the help of Nicotine Anonymous. But today I do see how far the town is and I am not dependent on nicotine to carry me there. I know that my Higher Power will show me the way. Today I trust my feelings instead of hiding from them.

Today, I rely on Nicotine Anonymous to showing me how to live without drug dependency. I rely on my Higher Power and trust my own feelings.

Only those who can see the invisible
can do the impossible.
—ALBERT EINSTEIN

When I am feeling the stress or pressure that used to drive me to nicotine, I remember that I have the power to choose a new response today.

I choose not to simply follow, and fall prey to, my initial emotional reaction to any outside stimulus or agitation. I ask myself whether I can control or change the situation or stressor. I choose to put things in the hands of my Higher Power, and I consider my part in making things better. No matter what may be happening outside of me, no matter what people may do and say, no one has the power to make me feel any particular emotion or feeling. No one can take away my freedom to step back and choose my response.

I see and hear people who react to every little stimulus and agitation. They seem to take it all upon themselves like bricks on their backs, weighing themselves down until they cannot stand it any longer, and must either find escape or collapse.

Today, I have the power to live differently. Through our Fellowship and with the strength of my Higher Power, I choose to live serenely and without the need of escape.

The ignorant man becomes angry.
The wise man understands.

—INDIAN PROVERB

One of the things I love about the serenity prayer is acceptance. It is such a profound concept. If I stop to accept that perhaps my way is not the only way, or that I have no control over others' behavior, my anger can dissipate and I can be more open and more accepting of a situation that initially makes me uncomfortable. I can "look for the lesson" in my feelings and begin to understand.

*Today, I will try to be more accepting so that
I can turn my anger into understanding.*

Sometimes in the winds of change we
find our true direction.
—MAC ANDERSON

I see my Higher Power as the very replacement over the kingship that
nicotine had in my life. After endless attempts to quit using by my
own power and good deeds, being Mr. Fellowship, starting meetings,
people pleasing, and caring what others think, I only fell flat on my face
by slipping again and again.

There came that day when I realized that all of my resources had
failed me. But, thank God, recovering members of our Program were
inspired to write a book. Page twelve of the original edition states, "a
return to nicotine was part of the process of hitting a real bottom."

Now, it does not tell me to go and feed my addiction, but it does say
I will learn more about my condition. Through the failures, I learned
that, left to my own power, I am destined to live in my addiction to the
bitter end. My Higher Power, my only defense to this deadly disease, has
now taken the throne. All I do is serve the Good King, take correction
and direction, and give what I can to my fellow sufferers.

*Today, I realize that I have no effective mental
defense against this disease. My King has done for
me what I could not do for myself.*

If you have the courage to begin,
you have the courage to succeed.

—DAVID VISCOTT

The last time I used nicotine, I had already gone nearly sixty days without feeding my addiction. Then came a craving. I sat at my kitchen table telling it to go away, and it said no. I knelt down and prayed, it still it said no. I went to a meeting, but still it said no. I called at least seven other nicotine addicts, but the craving continued to say, "no way." I did everything humanly possible to be rid of that relentless craving. Nothing worked. My addiction won.

However, I learned a valuable lesson. I realized I was still trying to control my addiction. I realized my best efforts left me with no defense from my addiction. I needed one hundred percent Divine help to stop. I finally and fully conceded my powerlessness over nicotine, and started letting God provide my defense.

I am now working Step Eight and Step Nine with my sponsor. I am allowing God and my sponsor to guide me to freedom from nicotine. If not for Nicotine Anonymous, I would still be a slave, worshipping nicotine as king.

*Today, I remember to surrender my
addiction to God, and I thank God for
keeping me on the path of joy and serenity.*

Take God out of the church and give him a home.
He will thank you and he will share his toys.
—LON SPIEGELMAN

The larger the grain of sand, the easier it is to handle. It is life's tiniest grains that seem to slip out of our control.

The only procrastination program that works in a positive manner is the one I used in relation to my nicotine addiction.

It is the Positive Procrastination Program, or PPP. When I get that craving for a cigarette, I utter the letters PPP and put off lighting up for a set period of time, usually a few minutes.

As I distanced myself in time from the initial craving, maybe two or three minutes of time, I forgot about lighting up until the next craving. As I continued to recover, I put several PPPs together until finally I was able to quit nicotine completely.

Today I remember to surrender my addiction
to God, and I thank God for keeping me on
the path of joy and serenity.

Great consolation may grow out
of the smallest saying.
—SWISS GERMAN PROVERB

When I was active in my addiction, I was caught up in a feeling that I needed lots more. Color me craving. Little would not do; a bunch was not enough, I needed lots. Having more than enough was a way to feel secure.

Once I got the craving chemical out of my body, I no longer had that panicky feeling. I will see how much I get from even the smallest of things. Also, without the continual panic that craving creates, I appreciate more what I have already.

In recovery I listen and read words that ease my anxieties, and relieve my despair. I find faith as I discover gems, even tucked away in tiny places and brief moments. When I take time to recall a Fellowship slogan, I find my day lightening, my spirit awakening, and my lungs expanding with an easier breath. This is enough.

Today, I am "grateful for grace," as well as
all those little things that so enlarge my life.

Without the acquisition of another skill, without
the acquisition of anything but complete and total
trust in God and in yourself, you have everything
you need to interact optimally, creatively and
productively with every situation you encounter.

—KEN CAREY

Oh, God of my understanding I pray, please give me whatever I
need to live this life free of tobacco.

For me tobacco is a poison I became addicted to. It ran my
life. I ask You, God, please help and guide me "one day at a time" in my
efforts to live free of my deadly addiction. This is the same addiction that
killed my mother in such an agonizing way. I truly believe in the core of
my being that Your will for me is to live free of the drug nicotine that I
used for so many years. Thank you, God for each and every moment free
of the compulsion to feed my addiction.

*Today, I know I can live free of nicotine as
long as I accept the help freely given to me by
my Higher Power.*

> Not everything that is faced can be changed, but
> nothing can be changed until it is faced.
> —JAMES A. BALDWIN

L iving free of tobacco addiction is the most important thing in my life. My life and my health depend on this. It is so vitally important for my spiritual growth, my physical being, my self-esteem, and my emotional center. I do not want to waste my life and my money by continuing an addiction that kills and maims addicts in the prime of our lives, and cuts us off from each other and our Higher Power.

Oh God, please help me live the Twelve Steps. Help me seek help for myself. Help me give help to other addicts. Help me truly live this life as You would have me live it. I pray to live "one day at a time" doing the "next right thing." Working our Twelve Steps helps me avoid physical, emotional and spiritual death, and I am grateful.

*Today, I know all that God asks is that
I "do the next right thing."*

We took a realistic look at the power nicotine had over
us, and we saw that its control was absolute.

—NICOTINE ANONYMOUS:THE BOOK

I smoked from infancy, inhaling second-hand smoke from both of my parents who were heavy smokers. I became addicted first hand when I was sixteen. I believed I could beat the odds and be a recreational, controlled smoker. Tobacco beat me every day. After 30 years of being a heavy smoker, and countless attempts at stopping, I found myself at Nicotine Anonymous meetings, continuing to smoke for months.

Then the miracle happened. I have not had tobacco or nicotine in any form for over four years.

I still attend meetings. I am so grateful to live nicotine-free "one day at a time." I believe praying for the willingness to quit, and doing the God work with my Higher Power's guidance through our Fellowship makes it possible for me to live nicotine-free.

*Today, I thank God and the Fellowship I found in Nicotine
Anonymous and for the miracle of living free.*

I realize I had been living a grand hoax.
I haven't given up anything at all.
—PROMISES OF NICOTINE ANONYMOUS

Nicotine limited me. I was enslaved. When I started smoking it was to be a part of, to join my peers. After thirty-five years, as a practicing addict, I was no longer accepted. My peers had quit. I felt like an outcast.

I lived in fear that I would be forced to be somewhere I could not smoke. Long plane flights were no longer possible.

I have been free of the compulsion to plan my life around my nicotine addiction for five years. I am free to go anywhere I want, and to stay as long as I want. I am free.

Today God, I choose the gift of living free of nicotine. God, don't let me forget the restrictions nicotine demanded in my life.

We knew we would have to quit the deadly business of
living alone with our conflicts, and in honesty confide
these to God and to another human being.
—ALCOHOLICS ANONYMOUS

I was having trouble sleeping; I just generally did not feel well. I had
been calling my sponsor every day for over five months, but I was
reluctant to let him know how I was really feeling. My sponsor had
the tendency to ask me to read the literature when I was not doing well,
and I did not want to bother with that.

Finally I leveled with my sponsor, who pointed out I was trying to
bargain with God. I was saying, "God, if you just let me have my way on
this one thing, I will continue to surrender to Your will for me." I was
refusing to surrender, and my sponsor told me I sounded quite
miserable. He was right. I was miserable, but wanted desperately to be
"happy, joyous and free." Instead of giving me the answers again, my
sponsor said the answer was in the book if I wanted to read it.

I was reminded I need to pray only for God's will, not mine, and
continue to pray throughout the day whenever I find myself insisting on
my way. I found relief.

*Today, I thank God for my sponsor and all those who
hold up a mirror so I can see myself as I truly am.*

> We relax and take it easy.
> We don't struggle.
>
> —ALCOHOLICS ANONYMOUS

I love the slogan "easy does it." It seems to be my nature to stress over life's everyday events. In the past, I thought chewing tobacco reduced my stress. Now I know nicotine addiction added to my stress levels, and pulled my self-esteem and feelings of security down.

I have also learned that sometimes I cannot help getting stressed. I feel my blood pressure rising as well as other stress-related symptoms, and want some relief. Often just repeating "easy does it" gives me the feeling some relief. I choose to remember that nothing is worth smoking over. Nothing. I remember that to go back to chewing over a stressful situation would become a permanent answer to a temporary problem.

Today, in any stressful situation, instead of reaching for nicotine, I will breathe deeply, think relaxing thoughts.

A moment's insight is sometimes
worth a life's experience.
—OLIVER WENDELL HOLMES

My part in recovery from nicotine addiction is and has been minimal compared to the part played by my Higher Power. My part was seeking, finding, calling on that Power, and acknowledging its source. I had proven I was powerless over my addiction by smoking three packs daily for forty-three years.

I had watched other addicts recover using Twelve Step Programs. I knew the Steps worked, and that God blesses those who sincerely try to live the Steps. I consulted God about His plans for me, and asked Him to direct some Power my way if His plans would be helped by my not smoking. I agreed to cooperate with the miracle by being willing to use any available aids. I agreed when we were successful that I would let everyone know about this special stop-smoking Power.

Recently I celebrated two years of a life free of nicotine. Just for fun, I have the opportunity to share my "experience, strength and hope" with others in the Nicotine Anonymous Fellowship.

Today, I thank God for the courage to change what I can, and the wisdom to rely on God for the rest.

> We are not cured.... What we really have is a daily
> reprieve contingent on the maintenance of our
> spiritual condition.
>
> —BILL W.

I never believed I could stop using nicotine. I made a few, pitiful attempts over the years, but I could not do it by myself. What was the problem? Was I so very weak or so very stubborn? Was it a lack of willpower? Or too much self-will? It did not matter. I was hopelessly stuck, afraid and imprisoned by nicotine.

I prayed for my Higher Power to help me. I read Alcoholics Anonymous' "Came to Believe," a book about how the obsession to use alcohol was removed from people by their Higher Power. I could not do this under my own power. Nicotine's control of me was absolute. And then, one morning, my nicotine obsession was lifted.

What a gift. To be free of this nightmare was a miracle. Part one was receiving the gift: part two is my maintaining this freedom by constant vigilance. I know where my freedom comes from. I thank my Higher Power and talk to Him each day; aim for a gratitude attitude; attend meetings; read Twelve Step literature, and share my "experience, strength and hope" with others. Life is so good without addiction, and I am willing to work every day to stay free.

Today, by the Grace of my Higher Power, I am free of nicotine. Please, help me to stay that way.

The only requirement for Nicotine Anonymous
membership is a desire to stop using nicotine.

—TRADITION THREE

When I first came to Nicotine Anonymous, I was still smoking. I quit then because I was worried about what the group thought of me. That was not a strong enough reason for me to continue to not smoke, because after twenty-nine days I started smoking again, and I stopped coming to meetings.

A year later, I returned. This time I was determined to surrender my addiction to God. It took me another fifteen months to learn how to let go. Tradition Three gave me permission to "keep coming back" to meetings so I could learn.

I did eventually learn to trust my Higher Power. I set my quit date. With God's help I became willing to endure, even to embrace, the cravings.

I kept coming back because I had to, and because Nicotine Anonymous said I could.

Today, I remember the words of Mother Teresa, "God does not call us to be successful. He calls us to be faithful."

The process of change is like planting a seed and
watching it grow and bloom into a flower.
—MELODY BEATTIE

O ne of the miracles that happened when I quit using nicotine was
that I learned to love myself. Without nicotine, I learned that I
had choices and I began doing what I needed to do for myself.
The road was not easy. I lost many friends along the way, friends who
did not like who I was becoming. But I replaced those friends with
people who genuinely love me for myself, not for what I am able to do
for them.

I learned that using nicotine did not reduce stress in my life. It
actually prolonged stress. Nicotine did not help me cope. Nicotine
trapped me in unhealthy behavior. After I quit, I became more aware of
my feelings and the choices available to me. I learned that going to
meetings and doing service kept me from picking up nicotine, "one day
at a time."

I learned to set goals. Before Nicotine Anonymous I demanded
instant gratification. Today, I am willing to wait and work towards my
goals. What a wonderful feeling that is.

*Today, I live in the present. I thank God that I am free to make
choices, set goals, and enjoy the present moment.*

> Having had a spiritual awakening as the
> result of these Steps, we tried to carry this
> message to nicotine users and to practice
> these principles in all our affairs.
>
> —STEP TWELVE

I was sitting in the lounge of another Twelve Step Program when a lady I knew posted a flier on the bulletin board. The flier asked the question, "Do you want to stop smoking?"

Not only did I want to stop smoking, I wanted to be able to stay stopped. I had stopped smoking over and over, only to return to the habit and addiction one more time.

I decided to go to the meeting. I wanted to be able to say I was a former smoker when I introduced myself for the first time, so I was nicotine-free for three days before the meeting. Through this Program, I learned to continue to live nicotine-free. Now I "carry the message" to other nicotine addicts who still suffer.

---

*Today, I allow life to flow through me
and to bless myself and others.*

Take a deep breath. Usually, we anticipate something to
follow that is painful, like a shot. Or maybe someone is
asking us to calm down. How about just for today, you say to
yourself, "take a deep breath." You don't have to have a
reason. But what a blessing a deep breath is.

—REV. JOEL HUGHES

Whenever I had to meet with people I did not know, I always
felt compelled to have to feed my nicotine addiction. As soon
as I had the first hit, my feeling of fear was subdued. I felt
more prepared to make acquaintances.

It bothered me that I had to depend on nicotine to make me feel
normal, to shrink my fear to a manageable level.

By coming to meetings and "working the Steps," I learned to love
myself. As I learned to love myself, I released my fear of meeting new
people. I also learned that not everyone will like me, and that's OK.

*Today, I thank God for lifting my fears and
allowing me to meet people without a drug.*

Nowhere can man find a quieter or more
untroubled retreat than in his own soul.
—MARCUS AURELIUS

E arlier in my life, I never thought of asking God to relieve me of
my obsession to use nicotine. It seemed very normal because so
many people I knew used nicotine in some form. Somewhere, it
quit seeming normal, people I knew were quitting.

Eventually I could not deny the dangers. The diseases caused by my
drug of choice are killers. I began to realize that I had to quit.

I found Nicotine Anonymous and the Twelve Steps. Prayer and
meditation bring me closer to my Higher Power, and help me on my
path to recovery.

Today, I thank God for helping me live nicotine-
free "one day at a time," for the rest of my life.

I am looking forward to today. There's a Nicotine
Anonymous meeting this evening.
—NICOTINE ANONYMOUS MEMBER

L ike many others in our Program, I could quit on my own, but
staying quit was impossible. Then I found Nicotine Anonymous.
Meetings were definitely the answer to my problem of
addiction. Being with others, and sharing our "experience, strength and
hope" turned my life around.

I thank God every day that I no longer have to feed my addiction. I
thank God for the Nicotine Anonymous Fellowship, because without
this Program I might return to living as an addict. I enjoy my life, and I
want to keep it like it is, free of nicotine.

*Today, I thank God for our Fellowship and
freedom from addiction.*

Man is made or unmade by himself. By the right
choice he ascends. As a being of power,
intelligence, and love, and the lord of his own
thoughts, he holds the key to every situation.

—JAMES ALLEN

Nicotine Anonymous has given me the desire to get well and to overcome my addiction. It gives me a sense of safety, a sense of fellowship and belonging.

Since I arrived at my first Nicotine Anonymous meeting, I haven't fed my addiction. When I first heard, "Keep Coming Back," my response was, "you betcha."

I love to share my "experience, strength and hope" with others. I also love to hear others share theirs. By going to meetings on a regular basis, I have learned to live life without my drug of choice, nicotine.

Whenever I see a newcomer at a meeting, I introduce myself, make sure they have a schedule of meetings, and always remind them to "Keep Coming Back."

*Today, I thank God for the Program and the Fellowship
that encourages me to "keep coming back."*

I am indeed a practical dreamer ... I want to convert my
dreams into realities as far as possible.
—MAHANDAS GANDI

I used to be enslaved by nicotine. That may sound like an exaggeration, but nicotine prevented me from knowing myself and doing what I really wanted to do in life. I was an addict. I smoked one to two packs a day for forty years.

I never felt I could rely on my own abilities. I needed something to alter my mood. I thought I could think better, write better, drive better, and talk more intelligently when I smoked.

The last twenty years of my addiction was spent in fear of the consequences, but also in fear of life without cigarettes. I was trapped.

Today, thanks to the Twelve Steps of Nicotine Anonymous and my group, I am a different person. I am free. I am free to pursue a life I could only dream about before.

Recently, I celebrated my sixth nicotine-free anniversary in a village in South Africa, helping teach English, science and math, and working on community development projects as a volunteer.

Today, I love what I am doing,
and I love being nicotine-free.

> If the doors of perception were cleansed the world
> would appear as it is, infinite.
>
> —WILLIAM BLAKE

L ife is a gift from my Higher Power. I never understood that when I was smoking. There was a constant depression, a denial of what I was doing to my being, a self-destructiveness that negated the gift.

Now that I have moved over to the other side, from death to life, I see. I can value the gift and take care of it. Life is worth living. The depression lifts or at least lessens. Instead of destructive behavior, I behave in physically life-enhancing activities like running, biking, and swimming, or annual medical check ups, eating and sleeping well.

I do not know how to explain to a nicotine addict what is on the other side of the door of addiction. But, if the door can be opened enough to glimpse the totally new orientation to life that is on the other side, then hope rather than despair is possible. There is a new freedom that is more than freedom from nicotine but also a freedom from the negative orientation to life that is the addict's lot.

Go through the door. It will hurt. There will be demons, temptations, and midnight struggles. But a Higher Power and friends in this Program will be there to help do what is impossible to do alone. I have heard the saying "Courage is fear that has said its prayers."

I have experienced a miracle.

*Today, I will open the doors of my fears with courage
and the support of my friends in the Program.*

The space for what you in your life is already
filled by what you settled for instead.

—GRACE TERRY

For twenty years I struggled to quit smoking, but I never could stay quit. Fourteen of those years were after part of my left lung was removed. Every time I quit it was progressively harder, physically and emotionally. Every time I quit, I did so for a shorter period. I did not believe I had another quit in me. And, I knew that if I tried again and failed again, I would die smoking. I was hopelessly addicted, and the addiction was gaining power.

Then my teenage son got involved with alcohol and drugs. Early in his treatment, he confronted me. He said that all his life, every morning, he would listen to my hacking. He had always been afraid I would die, and he would have no one. How could I have been so blind to the damage I had been doing to my beloved, only child?

I found Nicotine Anonymous. You showed me the lies about nicotine. You were happy to live without nicotine. I learned to stop for a moment of truth every time I saw someone else smoking. Rather than being jealous because, "they can smoke and I can't," I learned to, "thank God I am free today." In a remarkably short time those words became a true expression, instead of a wish.

Today, I am grateful to be alive, happy,
and healthy. I love life and life is great.

The only thing we have to fear is fear itself—nameless,
unreasoning, unjustified terror—which paralyzes
needed efforts to convert retreat into advance.
—FRANKLIN D. ROOSEVELT

I treated feelings like facts, so the only way to find relief was through
my nicotine addiction. You showed me the only power and reality
behind my feelings is what I grant them. I learned to honor my
feelings and to search for the lessons behind them. I learned to change
what I could. I learned about boundaries, setting and enforcing my own,
and respecting boundaries set by others for themselves.

Yesterday, I struggled to fight through fears. If something was hard, I
just had to be tougher. Nicotine Anonymous taught me to, "let go and let
God." Today, I am learning to gently release fears in all areas of my life. I
am learning to reinforce a new vision for myself, instead of fighting
against the old behaviors.

Instead of affirming, "I am terrified to sing publicly," I affirm, "God
gave me talent I am delighted to share." Instead of affirming, "I am
terrified of heights," I affirm, "I am free to enjoy heights." All statements
are expressions of feelings. None is a fact. I am free to choose the one I
want for my truth.

*Today, I take care in choosing the words that follow,
"I am." I know those words will be my truth.*

Fear is a tyrant and a despot, more terrible than
the rack, more potent than the snake.

—EDGAR WALLACE

When I was a toddler, I climbed up on a desk, picked up my dad's magazine, and leaned up against the screen to read it. The screen came loose, and I fell backwards out of the second story window. I have always been sure that caused my fear of heights. That fear kept me from doing things I thought looked like fun for others. I had to avoid things like ski lifts and hot air balloon rides. I always said that someday, I would work on getting over my fear.

Then one day I realized that I affirmed my fear, gave it power and permanence, every time I said or thought, "I am afraid of heights." I changed and began affirming that I have released my fear. I bought a model of a hot air balloon, and put it in my office to remind me to affirm, "I am free to enjoy heights."

That's all I did. I did not go to a counselor to learn how to adjust to my fear, or to work through the panic. I simply affirmed my new freedom.

A few days later, I had the opportunity to test my freedom. My husband actually challenged me to test myself. I affirmed my freedom, then I looked down. There was no panic, only a slight flutter. I chose to attribute the flutter to the awesome view.

Today, I acknowledge my feeling of fear; I decide
whether the feeling is still useful to me, and if not,
I gently release it and affirm my new choice.

We are also beginning to love ourselves.

—ALCOHOLICS ANONYMOUS

During the changing seasons it is apparent a Higher Power is at work in the world. I need to realize there is a Higher Power at work in me as well. I am a unique being to be cherished. I did not come off of some celestial assembly line but was made special and unique.

It is often too easy for me to see myself as unwanted goods. Whether it is because I have been hurt growing up or just have a low self-image I have been accustomed to think of myself as "less than."

That is one reason I used nicotine, to blot out the feelings of discomfort I felt in my own skin.

The beauty of the Twelve Steps is that they help me come to know myself again, in the way my Higher Power knows and loves me. I have found the best tool is the Fourth Step inventory. I was tempted to list only the areas I am lacking, but the Fourth Step is truly meant to be a way to take stock of my whole self. I must not list only my liabilities; I must list my assets as well. I was surprised to find there are many. It is essential to know what a precious, unique person I am and to see my place in this wonderful creation.

*Today, I thank my Higher Power for creating
me as a unique and essential person.
I love me as you love me.*

There is nothing permanent except change.

—HERACLITUS

I do not like change. As a nicotine addict, change can be completely devastating for me. When change comes into my life, whether I have invited it in or it is knocking down the door uninvited, I lose the sense of control that seems essential to my being. I feel best when I am in control and change embodies a total lack of control.

During times of change I need to remember the Serenity Prayer, "God, grant me the serenity to accept the things I cannot change." I do not really have any power over the direction my life goes, even when I believe I am in control. But no matter what path my life takes, my Higher Power is always there to hold my hand and to guide me.

"Living life on life's terms" is a good philosophy to practice. It is an acceptance of whatever turn my life seems to make. When I accept it rather than fight it, I find I enjoy my path so much more and serenity really can find a place in my heart. Fortunately for me, change, good and bad, is part of the journey of recovery. Whatever shape it takes, it molds me into the new person I am becoming.

Today, I thank God for giving me the
courage to change with serenity.

Sought through prayer and meditation to improve my
conscious contact with God as I understand Him.

—STEP ELEVEN

P racticing my daily meditation is very important to me, but it is not
always easy. I get a little annoyed sometimes. "Yup. Okay. I get it.
Time to gently release the thought and bring my attention back to
my breathing, again." Ugh.

Today, my mind was diving and tunneling and leaping all over the
map. It reminded of the way my cats love to jump suddenly and dart
around. I was watching my mind frolic and play. My face broke out into
a big stupid grin, and I started laughing under my breath. If you have
done much meditating in groups, or if you have spent any time talking to
your best friend in school during class, you will know what it was like. It
was great to stop taking myself so seriously, and to let meditating be fun.

For me, that was enlightenment, to notice how funny I can be, and
to laugh at myself. I decided that, "the sound of one hand clapping" is
the sound of my hand clapping over my mouth to stifle my laughter.
Maybe Bodhidarma would not have approved, but it was good enough
for me.

Nicotine Anonymous has taught me that "surrender allows change."
If I "keep showing up" and working my Program, my life just keeps
getting better.

*Today, I thank God for life's everyday pleasures,
and for granting me the wisdom to see them.*

As long as you "keep showing
up," you haven't given up.

—NICOTINE ANONYMOUS MEMBER

Fellowship with other recovering nicotine addicts demonstrates the presence of a loving Higher Power. At meetings people welcomed me every time I showed up, even while I was still active in my addiction. They understood my struggle. They did not judge or criticize. They hugged me and smiled. They told me to "keep coming back."

It was their love and understanding that gave me the strength to keep getting back in my car and coming to meetings even when I felt hopeless. Their voices in my head, my memory of their warmth and caring, were what enabled me to pick up the telephone and call for help. Whether it was to seek help when I was craving a cigarette, or to confess that I had failed again, or to get support so I would resist picking up, there was always someone who had the time to talk.

I kept coming back, and today I am free of the compulsion to feed my nicotine addiction.

Today, I will accept each person I encounter with the unconditional love I have learned in our Program.

> I must be an addict because after sixteen
> years of not smoking, I become very angry
> when I am in a room with smokers.
> —NICOTINE ANONYMOUS MEMBER

Sometimes I think that I am not addicted to the nicotine in cigarettes. After all, I did not start smoking until I was forty years old, and stopped after ten years. Okay, it took three attempts to quit during that decade.

The first time I relapsed I smoked for six months; the second relapse lasted thirteen months. The third time I quit smoking, I made it to my first Nicotine Anonymous meeting at that critical time of six months. That was three years ago.

What reminds me that I am an addict is that smokers fascinate me.

When I see someone smoking in a car or on the street, I want a cigarette. Then I hear the honesty of another member sharing and I remember that I am an addict and I have a daily reprieve.

I "keep coming back" to remember I am an addict.

---

*Today, I thank God I recognize my addiction and am willing
to choose to abstain from feeding that addiction.*

Today is the beginning of a wonderful day until
someone comes and messes it up.

—UNKNOWN

I discovered this truthful saying on a piece of china and it really made me think. It does not always have to be someone else but can actually be me who ruins the day. I am the king of self-deception, and not only that, but I also believe my own tricks which are tangled up with problems that I wrote, directed, produced and starred in. In the end I blame everyone else except myself, thus falling in the trap of "poor lil' ole me."

At moments like that, I can remember the Serenity Prayer and put myself in His hands (Step Three). "The Boss" (my God) is the only one who really knows what will happen and I am only a small instrument of His will trying to achieve, although I do not always succeed, my "day by day."

Today, I will pause and look at what I
am doing to create discomfort.

As long as I am working on quitting smoking, my
Higher Power will take care of everything else.
—NICOTINE ANONYMOUS MEMBER

In the beginning, just staying off nicotine is hard enough. So I have to let my Higher Power handle whatever else comes along. As the days pass and my emotions settle down and the cravings lessen, then I can think about what else I need to be doing, like "working the Steps," and deepening my contact with my Higher Power.

*Today, Higher Power, thanks for watching over my life
and supporting me in my desire to overcome nicotine.*

Admitted I am powerless over nicotine, that my
life had become unmanageable.
—STEP ONE

In June 1978 I was trying, again, to quit using nicotine. That time I was using an aid, a type of filter system. A friend was quitting with me, so I had some support.

On the thirtieth of that month, I was down to the fourth filter. That day I wound up at the hospital because I could not breathe and was in severe pain. My doctor said I had pneumonia in my right lung, and my left lung was partially collapsed. I had to be hospitalized, and could not even go home to pack a bag. He sent me to have some lunch while I waited for the thoracic surgeon to be available to see me.

First I had a cigarette with a filter. Then I decided I needed more nicotine so I covered the hole in the filter. Then I pulled off the filter and just smoked. In that hour, I chain smoked most of a pack. I was gasping for breath. I was turning blue from lack of oxygen. Still the most important thing to me was feeding my addiction.

I did not get to Nicotine Anonymous for another fourteen and a half years. For all those years, I believed that nicotine was the only thing that made my life possible. I knew I was addicted, that was why I had not quit. Until I got to Nicotine Anonymous, I had not admitted my life was unmanageable. Step One has two parts, and both are vitally important to my recovery.

*Today, every time I see another nicotine addict, I take
time to thank God I am "happy, joyous and free."*

"A Puff Away From a Pack a Day"
—NICOTINE ANONYMOUS SLOGAN

I like to remember that my addiction is ever present, that I am only a "puff away from a pack a day." It keeps me humble, and helps me remember how powerless I am over this addiction.

Today, Higher Power, help me to remember that I am powerless over nicotine and that with your help I will be thankful for each day without nicotine.

It is never too late to become
what you might have been.

—GEORGE ELIOT

One of the things I have noticed at Nicotine Anonymous meetings is how many people cough. And we all know about "smoker's cough." It's actually a good thing: it's our lungs trying desperately to clear themselves of all the toxins from cigarettes.

When I went to an annual Nicotine Anonymous conference, I noticed there was no coughing in the room. Some of those people have not had a cigarette in many years. How wonderful that we have that to look forward to.

*Today, I thank my Higher Power for
helping me to have healthy lungs.*

When health is absent, wisdom cannot reveal itself, art
cannot manifest, strength cannot fight, wealth becomes
useless, and intelligence cannot be applied.

—HEROPHILUS

Last night I got a beautiful night's sleep. I went to bed at the right time for me to get the rest I needed. I felt vigorous and energetictoday. I had the extra zing to go on an extra errand for myself, an outing that was frivolous and fun, beyond the demands of a very full day.

Did I believe the idea that staying up nights was proof of my sophistication? This need to show the world that I was cool led to a whole set of activities that seem somehow related. For me, nicotine was the addictive core. For others, additional addictions might have been involved. It seems that habits and attitudes fell into place to sustain and protect the addiction. Now I look back and see these choices as poor decisions made by an immature teenager. The problem is that I continued to live out those choices for many, many years after.

What did I gain by staying up late, and dragging through the next day exhausted? Was I automatically part of the crowd who stayed up to watch the same silly TV show? Maybe that was important to me as a teenager. For me now, I am pleased when I feel well rested. My nerves are not on edge and things go much more smoothly. My thinking is affected by how well I feel. When I am tempted to make a nasty remark or to show irritability, let me stop and check the source of my short temper.

Today, I resolve to take very good care
of myself.

> The most powerful agent of growth and
> transformation is something much more basic than
> any technique: a change of heart.
>
> —JOHN WELWOOD

Those horrible "afters." I am constantly reminded of all the times I smoked: after using the phone, after a meal, after sex. What do I do now?

I have to remember that abstinence is a minute-by-minute, hour-by-hour, day-by-day experience: "one day at a time." Also I recall that "the craving will pass whether I smoke or not." A craving is simply my body telling me it is time to put a call in to my Higher Power.

Today, I will call on my Higher Power to stay with
me and support me when I want to smoke.

The only source of knowledge is experience.

—ALBERT EINSTEIN

Eventually the craving for nicotine begins to pass the further away I am from my quit date. I have gone through those intense emotions and I actually have begun to forget about nicotine sometimes. This is the time when I can be present, instead of wondering when the next hit will be.

The thing about being present is that I get to enjoy all the wonderful things that are happening around me every day.

Today, I take time to express my gratitude to my Higher Power. Thank you for easing my cravings and giving me the opportunity to experience life today.

We have enormous power in knowing
the truth of our own experience.
—ANITA HILL

I stopped using nicotine because I knew it was killing me. My friends and family may have tried to get me to quit, but until I was ready, it was not going to happen. Sometimes my addict friends do not believe I will stay quit. I have to trust my own experience and my own Higher Power in regard to my addiction.

*Today, I trust my own experience and use it as a
teacher in working with my addiction.*

"The craving will pass whether you smoke
or not."
—NICOTINE ANONYMOUS MEMBER

I can remember when I was a nicotine user. I would always say to myself, "One more and then I will go to sleep," "one more and then I'll go to bed." A half a pack later, I would finally go to bed without a thought of what I must smell like, or that I just washed my hair and brushed my teeth. I never thought of my poor, non-smoking husband.

Today, I cannot stand the smell of smoke. I can tell a smoker if they walk past me, even if they are not smoking.

Since coming to Nicotine Anonymous I finally have self-respect. I finally have what I needed, a group of people who want to share about nicotine addiction.

Today, I ask you Lord, help me stay nicotine-free. Thank you for restoring my senses.

Some people change when they see the light,
others when they feel the heat.

—CAROLINE SCHOEDER

When I found Nicotine Anonymous, I was taking care of my Mother who was dying from emphysema. I was also suffering from emphysema in earlier stages. I came to meetings for months, but still struggled to quit. I got a sponsor, then I got a second sponsor, and still I struggled.

Finally one day, I was at the emergency room because my bronchitis was so bad I could not breathe. While I waited, I wrote in my journal. I wrote that nicotine was my only connection to normalcy, to health, to sociability. For the first time, I realized how much power I had given to nicotine, and just how insane I had become.

I continued to give in and smoke. I still thought that just the next cigarette was not so bad. Eventually I was ready to face reality. I was ready to accept cravings, knowing they are feelings, not facts, and that they would pass if I just did not continue to feed my addiction.

Today, I thank God for the Fellowship of Nicotine Anonymous, all those members who loved and accepted me through my struggle to recovery.

We don't know exactly how our dream will be
accomplished. We don't even know if it's probable. But
we can believe that with God's help it is possible.
—MARY MANIN MORRESSEY

I was down and out, in a lot of trouble physically and mentally. There was no way that continuing to smoke was going to work for me. My doctors warned me about lung cancer. They removed part of my lung. I still had a desire to smoke. Instead, I went back to Nicotine Anonymous where I received encouragement from my group.

Today, I do not need to smoke and have no desire to. I keep going to meetings. Maybe my story will help somebody. I will always be grateful to my local meeting and the Program because I was told to "keep coming back" and that the Program would eventually "get" me. It did.

*Today. I ask myself what I can do to
give back to my meeting.*

Live today as if there were no tomorrow and the
present is yours forever.
—JEAN MANTHEI

Some of the tools I have discovered are: my Higher Power, meditation, staying with the urge and riding it out, accepting discomfort, and the "five D's"—deep breath, distract, delay, do something else, and drink water. I do what works for me, not what I think I should or must do. I have found that the biggest reasons I relapsed was that I did not use my own coping strategies, including prayer.

Finding the peace that knows no understanding comes with acceptance and love of others and myself. The gains of recovery far outweigh the costs and pain of using nicotine and relapsing. I focus on the fact that, yes, there will be moments of discomfort, but also that there will be more laughter, love, affection, creativity, joy, increased control, greater self-esteem, and other feelings of all kinds. Are these not more desirable than the self-abuse suffered from the choice to use nicotine, and the resulting sense of despair and hopelessness?

*Today, I will continue my recovery by accepting discomfort
and opening myself to a greater goodness.*

MARCH 10

Teams share the burden and divide the grief.
—DOUG SMITH

Having been nicotine-free for over eleven months, I was anxious to reach the one-year plateau. I continued to do the things that had gotten me to that point: asking God for help; talking with other addicts; going to meetings; and thanking God at night for another day of freedom from my addictions.

One night, however, I had a strange dream. In the dream someone gave me a few dollars to get them something. I went to the store and bought a pack of cigarettes for myself. Without another thought I returned to my friend. Only then did I realize what I had done.

Now, I did not smoke any cigarettes, but I was awed at the ease and thoughtlessness with which I had purchased them.

The dream made me think how that kind of thing had happened to other members, some with a lot of clean time, who had gone back to nicotine with little or no forethought at all. Or of some who had mistakenly convinced themselves that they could just have one. I must always remember that it is not how much clean time I have; it staying clean today; and today is so very, very precious.

Today, I ask God to guide me and strengthen me
to stay clean just for these twenty-four hours.

There are two ways to live your life—one is as
though nothing is a miracle, the other is as though
everything is a miracle.

—ALBERT EINSTEIN

As a nicotine user I thought that the only way I would be able to stop living in my addiction would be by Divine intervention. I thought that some day the craving to use nicotine would be lifted and I would easily stop.

Upon entering Nicotine Anonymous, one of my early thoughts was that Divine intervention did not do it, but that Nicotine Anonymous did, and that I could accept the craving and not act on it.

After a little more time free from nicotine, I realized that it was a Higher Power that led me to Nicotine Anonymous, and that I had to "let go and let God" run my life.

*Today, I acknowledge God's presence in my life, and I
am grateful to surrender my will and my life.*

When your world is shaking and you are praying that
the world will stop shaking, consider that maybe your
Higher Power is doing the shaking.

—NICOTINE ANONYMOUS MEMBER

In my smoking days, I would get bronchitis at least once every winter, and when it got bad enough I would go to the doctor for antibiotics. At the clinic, there would always be a different doctor who would give me a lecture that went something like this:

"Your smoking is causing bronchitis and I can see by your chart that you get it at least once every year. I encourage you to stop smoking before you do more serious damage to your health."

I would walk out of the clinic, angry because a young doctor had lectured me again, and telling myself that of course smoking was not causing my bronchitis. I would light up a cigarette and cough some more. But I can tell you today that I have not had bronchitis once in the years since I quit smoking.

*Today, I pray that when my Higher Power shows
me a truth I can hear it and believe it.*

You are the only person God had in mind in
choosing you to be you.

—REV. JOEL HUGHES

For so many years, I punished myself for smoking and for being so
helpless over the addiction, making myself feel puny and
worthless. For years I would mentally beat myself. Even with
years in recovery, if I am not careful, I still punish myself. I do not beat
myself up about smoking anymore, but about other imagined
imperfections.

"Be good to yourself," I heard people I met saying at meetings.
"Rejoice in all the good we do and know that we are trying our best." I
have learned that if I make it through today nicotine-free my day is a
success, and that I have Step Ten to help make amends when needed.

I am learning to reward myself: a two week vacation in Hawaii paid
for with money not spent on nicotine for one year; some quiet time with
the God of my understanding; feeling gratitude for being alive and
nicotine-free; staying after Nicotine Anonymous meetings and visiting
with people; being a sponsor; being sponsored. Even though being good
to myself seems hard to do when I need it the most, it is so important
and freeing and it makes me smile.

*Today, I will remember that I am not intended to
be perfect. Throughout the day I will find ways to
reward myself and be good to myself.*

I no longer search for "truth." I search only for
beliefs that serve me, that help me to get where I
truly want to go. Then I work diligently at
discarding beliefs that work against me.

—BARRY NEIL KAUFMAN

For me, the best gift of recovery is a true and honest relationship
with God as I understand God. I struggled with that before
recovery. I lived my life alone with no spiritual connections of any
personal meaning. And then people in recovery suggested that I develop
my own concept of God.

On a good day I do as suggested in our Twelve Steps, praying only
for God's will and the power and willingness to carry that out. Not
smoking or using nicotine, I believe, is God's will for me, as well as
trying in my own ways to "carry the message" of recovery.

To me, God is my partner in life. I do not claim to understand who
God is or how God works. This great mystery is my partner, my guide,
and my trusted helper.

*Today, I pray for and act in the faith that God
wants me to be "happy, joyous and free."*

We became willing to give up the notion of
controlling the use of nicotine.
—NICOTINE ANONYMOUS:THE BOOK

I learned the hard way about becoming a nicotine addict. I thought it was other people who got hooked, not me. I thought I could take it or leave it. But I always wanted more and soon craved nicotine when I did not smoke. When I tried to quit, I didn't like the feelings I later learned were the result of withdrawal.

Sometimes I would make it nicotine-free a couple of weeks. Then I would break down and have just one. After that first cigarette, my addiction was activated and I was powerless. I was back to craving cigarettes by the carton. My willpower was gone.

Finally I learned that it was the first one that hooked me. It is not the second or third or hundredth hit that does the damage. It is the first one; that first hit. Through the process of becoming willing, I have learned that no matter how compelling the thought of just one jolt of nicotine, the urge will pass and that I be free of nicotine "one day at a time."

Today, I remember that I have chosen to live free of the hideous nicotine addiction. It is the right choice for me.

Free at last, free at last. Thank God
Almighty, I'm free at last.
—MARTIN LUTHER KING, JR.

I used to believe I was free. I had learned to let go of other addictions. Then one day I realized my nicotine use was another addiction. Using nicotine was cutting me off from a true and personal relationship with God, a relationship based on freedom.

I had tried to quit since high school. I was varsity football and basketball, but could not run the one-mile track event because of my breathing. From age sixteen to fifty-eight, I attempted to quit many times, using many different methods, but never could stop for very long.

Then, I remembered the Twelve Step solution that had freed me from other addictions. I thought that maybe I could quit by applying those same principles to nicotine. Gathering the available information, I started a meeting for nicotine addicts on March 16, 1987, the date of my last cigarette. Nicotine Anonymous truly set me free. I now really know what Martin Luther King, Jr. meant.

Today, I thank God for guiding me
to true freedom.

We are as sick as our secrets.
—TWELVE STEP SAYING

One thing we learn in Nicotine Anonymous is to be honest with ourselves and with each other. We learn to do this because we find that keeping secrets keep us sick and not making progress in our recovery.

For most of us it takes time to become entirely honest, but it is always worth the effort. We do this by completing our Fourth Step inventory, and telling God and another human being our innermost secrets in Step Five. From this experience, we learn to be honest in life on a daily basis.

My experience with becoming honest is such that now when I start keeping secrets, I know I am deviating from my recovery and the Twelve Steps. Thoughts and behaviors I want to hide from friends and sponsors serve as a warning to me, threatening my recovery. If I cannot learn what is my truth and have the courage to accept it, I will become sick. My health is important to me, and the tools of the Program help keep that a priority in my recovery.

*Today, I remember that rigorous honesty is
the best health insurance policy.*

Came to believe that a Power greater than
ourselves could restore us to sanity.
—STEP TWO

Feeling grateful that I am an ex-smoker for some years now keeps me going when I wake up from a smoking dream or see someone puffing away on a nice summer day. One tool I use is to say, "God, I pray for that person," each time I notice someone smoking. It helps me not feel deprived.

I always need to remember that I gratefully chose not to smoke; no one is depriving me. Smoking is my enemy, never my friend. Nicotine use is always the problem, never the solution. Health is so precious and not smoking is good for my health.

Not smoking is a miracle for an addict like me, and I thank my Higher Power for this gift. Though I avoid nicotine use these days, I feel tremendous compassion for the nicotine addict who still suffers, and recovering addicts who still get the urge.

Today, I gratefully choose
freedom from addiction.

This above all: to thine ownself be true, and it
must follow, as the night the day, thou canst not
then be false to any man.

—WILLIAM SHAKESPEARE

Before I started coming to Nicotine Anonymous meetings, I was a
very dishonest person. I wanted everyone to like me, so I
pretended to agree with every thing they said. I would draw
harder on my cigarette to keep from saying how I really felt.

When I quit smoking, I had no place for these feelings to go. I was
very difficult and too blunt.

Because of Nicotine Anonymous, I learned to be honest and kind.
I'm not perfect, however I am a much happier person. Being able to tell
the truth with love makes me feel better about myself.

Today, I will remember that
honesty brings serenity.

All our life is but the blink of an eye.

—RAMAYANA

I think of all the people who have gone before us on this earth, and yet it is as if they were never here at all. They left no lasting impression. I think back to when I was actively practicing my addiction; it was the same with me; I wasn't really here at all.

Among the many gifts of the Program has been a greater awareness and appreciation for the daily experience of what is life. I no longer have to buffer this experience with the drug of nicotine.

Seeing things more clearly, as they truly are and not as I would like them continues to be a challenge; one that can be lived best without nicotine.

Today. I simply appreciate
each unfolding moment of life.

You will love again the stranger
who was yourself.
—DEREK WALCOTT

B y the time I had smoked for thirty years I had pretty much lost contact with who I really was. Anything genuine about myself had long been buried under a blanket of cigarette smoke.

Even now, as I begin to see more clearly, I realize that many of my earlier loves were put aside, everything from poetry to bowling, so that I could make room for how I ought to be. Using nicotine helped me do that.

Freedom from nicotine has led to greater freedom in all aspects of living. Old interests have been revived and new ones found as well.

Today, my goal in life is to become the best person I am capable of being.

Many people have found a strength far beyond
their own by relying on a Power greater than
themselves.

—ALCOHOLICS ANONYMOUS

Before coming to Nicotine Anonymous, I had tried on my own to quit smoking for twenty-five years. I guess I had to admit one hundred percent that without help quitting was too much for me. Then I could ask for help from others who had struggled as I had and who have been able to live nicotine-free.

With the "experience, strength and hope" shared from the group, I started to try again to quit. Still I did not have enough power. I learned that when I put out my last cigarette I knew that my faith in the power of my God would be the power I needed.

In the process of quitting I gave up many times each day. But each morning and each craving I asked my God to help me not to smoke no matter what. The help came when I surrendered and God answered my prayer by doing for me what I could not do for myself.

Without the love and support of Nicotine Anonymous and my Higher Power, quitting using nicotine and living life is too much for me.

*Today, I am grateful for the love and support of
Nicotine Anonymous and my Higher Power as I
accept all that life presents to me.*

Your end is your beginning, you
start when you finish.
—RAMAYANA

After thirty years of addiction, and seven years nicotine-free, I still remember my last smoke. I remember frantically smoking that butt before a Nicotine Anonymous meeting, and burning my lip in the process.

I can think of nothing positive that came from all those years of smoking. I have truly had an awakening, or a new way of life since then, living each day, "one day at a time," without nicotine.

It is refreshing to end one chapter, and to begin another. Having ended my smoking career, I discovered a full and rewarding life awaiting me, with no place for nicotine.

Today, I no longer have time to feed my nicotine addiction. I am free to enjoy all of life's pleasures.

To know even one life has breathed easier because
you have lived, this is to have succeeded.
—RALPH WALDO EMERSON

I had to finally get honest. I really did not want to quit smoking. So I decided to ask my Higher Power for the willingness to want to quit. My Higher Power granted me willingness quickly in the form of my inability to breathe and having to be rushed to the emergency room. The ER doctor said in front of my kids, "Did you know you're killing yourself in front of your kids? This is all cigarette-related. You wouldn't even be here if you didn't smoke."

My willingness came to me: I did not want to die. I did want to live. I became honest and in that honesty came freedom. It opened my eyes heart to reality and gave me willingness to get help for myself. Thank goodness for my Higher Power and for honesty as I am now a grateful recovering nicotine addict.

Today, I know that honesty can bring many rewards and one of those rewards is living without active addiction.

People who work together will win, whether it be
against complex football defenses, or the problems
of modern society."

—VINCE LOMBARDI

O ver twenty years ago, the last thing I wanted to do was to go to
Alcoholic Anonymous meetings. I thought I could handle it on
my own. I found out that I could not do it on my own. But I
went. Alcoholics Anonymous has given me nineteen years of sobriety.
Thank God and the Program.

When I wanted to quit using nicotine, for some dumb unknown
reason, the last thing I wanted to do was to go to a Nicotine Anonymous
meeting. So, on March 19, 2001 I quit again. I lasted about two weeks.
On March 25, 2001 I stopped again, this time using Nicotine
Anonymous.

The Programs are the same, only different. I gave my nicotine
addiction to God. The craving has disappeared. The urge to use nicotine
will stay away if I continue going to meetings. Quitting using nicotine
has been the frosting on my cake.

*Today, I am sensitive to resistance. If I feel resistance, I will stop to
consider what I need to release or what support I require.*

The [Fourth Step] inventory, though sometimes
painful, unlocks many of the secrets that keep us
prisoner and protect our addiction.
—TWELVE STEPS FOR TOBACCO USERS

Like many others, I had to have someone to blame for my
addiction. "If he would only stop _____ I could quit for good."
And so on. The trouble is I will always run into problems in my
life that seem insurmountable. Until I realize I am powerless over other
people, places and things, I am cut off from freedom.

Until I did a seriously thorough and courageous Fourth Step,
looking at all of my struggles in life and sorting out which ones I helped
cause, I could not be free. Freedom does indeed come from
wholeheartedly "working the Steps."

We may all have resentments, misgivings, things that make us wish
we were elsewhere or somebody else. If I faithfully turn to my Higher
Power for the lifting of these grievances, I will get answers. Prayer, if
given enough focus, can release me from the pain of my problems.

*Today, although it is tough for me as an addict to refrain from
blaming others, I take responsibility for my own actions.*

> Often the search proves more
> profitable than the goal.
> —E. L. KONIGSBURG

M y Higher Power is always available to me. When I am angry or frustrated, I can take the time to notice that I cannot change the situation or person on which I am focusing anger. Then I can "let go and let God" take care of it. I do not have the energy to fix everything. I want to be free to enjoy the wonders of life.

I can let my Higher Power decide how things will turn out. I can let myself be soft, open to God's will and be gentle with myself. I can relax into God's loving care.

If I want relief about something today, I can let God help me. I can remember that I am powerless over nicotine and ask for my Higher Power's guidance, comfort and wisdom.

Today, I will open my clenched hands
to receive God's love and help.

Many strokes will bring down the tallest tree.
—DAILY REFLECTIONS: A BOOK OF REFLECTIONS
BY A.A. MEMBERS

To help myself quit chewing, I made myself three easy goals to reach: short, medium and long-range goals.

I started going one hour without nicotine, then two hours, and then the long-range goal of four hours. I did this several times a day.

As my need for nicotine lessened, I would increase my goals, first by doubling the hours, then by days, weeks, months, until I was free of my desire for nicotine "one day at a time."

Today, I remember that when I "keep it simple," I can achieve my goals.

The central fact of our lives today is the absolute
certainty that our Creator has entered into our
hearts and lives in a way which is indeed
miraculous. He has commenced to accomplish
those things for us which we could never do by
ourselves.

—ALCOHOLICS ANONYMOUS

Giving anything up to my Higher Power was never an idea for
me. But since I came to the rooms of Nicotine Anonymous, I
have learned a new concept. I "made a decision to turn my will
and my life over to the care of God, as I understood Him" (Step Three).

One evening I was tired of feeling so bad and of coughing my head
off every morning. I knew I had to do something. For me, the only way
to quit using nicotine was to "turn it over" to my Higher Power. I was
alone and had gotten rid of all nicotine items around me. I walked out to
my pool. I held my hands up to my Higher Power. I prayed, "God, I'm
powerless over nicotine. Please take the desire to smoke away. I have
smoked for thirty-three years. I am powerless. Take it God." Then I
jumped into my pool.

When I came up to the surface, I felt like a cleansing had happened
and I felt deep inside of me that I really had no desire to smoke. Today
and every day I am a grateful recovering nicotine addict, thanks to my
Higher Power.

*Today, instead of trying to figure things out by myself, I
will try letting my Higher Power help me.*

Quitting smoking is the best gift
you can give yourself.

—NICOTINE ANONYMOUS MEMBER

I am learning to be patient with myself. I am learning that it does not help to beat myself for all the years I smoked because I cannot bring them back. All I have is today.

I have learned to love myself, more than I have ever loved myself before. I do nice things for myself, like taking a walk no matter the weather, taking a bubble bath, eating well and getting a decent night's sleep, or eating vegetables with dip.

I am learning to listen, to open my ears. I heard people in Nicotine Anonymous meetings rooting for me. I can be an example too by not smoking. Living free of nicotine has not been a painless or easy journey, but it has been a road very worth taking.

Today, I will appreciate my gifts and "carry the message" by living by example.

At the great heart of humanity, there is a deep
homesickness that never has been and never can be
satisfied with anything less than a clear, vivid
consciousness of the indwelling presence of God.

—DR. EMILY CADY

When the craving for nicotine hits, what is it really about? If I really listen with my heart I begin to realize what it is saying to me.

Is it not really a craving for closeness and intimacy with others? Is it not a yearning to be spiritually one with a Power greater than myself? And is it not a heartfelt plea to have a sense of belonging with others?

When the pain of craving comes, I choose to embrace myself instead of the spiritual death that comes from using nicotine.

Today, I will listen to what the craving is saying to me. I will not turn away from it; I will answer it. I will cultivate the courage to love.

By the yard it's hard, by the inch it's a cinch.

—BEN JOHNSON

Lack of power; that was my dilemma. I was a slave to an addiction I had no control over. The answer to this dilemma lay in my admission that I could not overcome this situation with my own resources; I needed help.

Not only did I need help from God, as I understood Him, but also from my fellow nicotine addicts who understood my powerlessness. This was the key for me, not only vertical help but horizontal help also, forming a cross of victory.

Through attending meetings, working the Twelve Steps and helping others, I have discovered the freedom I so desperately sought. I know this is possible for others too.

Today, freedom is mine if I ask for help from the God of my understanding and from my fellow recovering addicts.

I am powerless over nicotine but
not over my responsible choices.
—NICOTINE ANONYMOUS MEMBER

I am finding that life is like a puzzle with which I need to patiently and gently try to fit the many different pieces (choices) together, instead of thinking I have found the correct piece and forcing the fit. Forcing can distort and damage the entire puzzle (my life). Forcing the fit was my practice before I discovered Nicotine Anonymous, and my life was unmanageable. I actually thought nicotine helped me make good decisions as I contemplated them in a drugged fog.

And, now, when I tentatively try a piece of the puzzle that to all appearance, in my estimable judgment, is wrong it invariably slides into place and the whole puzzle is improved and harmonious, and I feel even more "happy, joyous and free."

This is why today I do not avoid or evade the inevitable puzzling circumstances of life. Instead, I welcome the challenge and am comfortable in the discomfort of seeking the right piece for the fitting solution, as I allow a Power greater than myself guide all my physical, mental, emotional and spiritual choices.

I am grateful that the daily polishing of my soul by practicing the Twelve Steps, Traditions and concepts in the Fellowship of Nicotine Anonymous has led me away from my addiction that clouded my soul and interfered with my Higher Power's will for me.

*Today, with the help of my Higher Power, I
can make responsible choices.*

Leap and the net will appear.

—JULIA CAMERON

When I tried to quit smoking, I would say things like, "well, I've cut down quite a bit," or "I am trying to quit," or "can I bum one of those? I am trying to quit." I tried to control nicotine by not using it as much. I tried to manage life without nicotine. Of course, those attempts were just that. I tried to quit. Have you ever tried to pick up a piece of paper? You either pick it up or you do not. It is the same thing with nicotine, I am either using it or I am not.

I sat on my bed late one night and the thought popped into my head, "if you want to quit smoking, you have got to quit smoking." Those of us who are in the grips of nicotine addiction will not laugh at this simple realization.

This time I simply surrendered; I just stopped fighting it. This time I stopped dwelling on the time since the last cigarette. I did not actually quit. I mean, I was just done. I was sick and tired of trying to defeat, control, or manage life without nicotine. This time, I am not tense about it. No longer does nicotine have its deadly grasp on my soul. No, it is not as though I have given up anything at all; I have just surrendered.

Today, if I am swimming against the tide of a situation and finding myself exhausted from the effort, I will try letting go and floating on the surface of the tide instead.

> Take a deep breath: it helps you pay attention. It's
> the miracle of our lives. There are always miracles
> going on, all we have to do is look for them.
> —NICOTINE ANONYMOUS MEMBER

Pausing in our hectic day to just take a breath and to pay attention helps reduce stress and remind us that our Higher Power is ever present. A deep breath is a miracle, as are so many things that are in our lives: a flower, a bee, a blade of grass. Sometimes just stopping to pay attention is all we need to see the miracles around us, and to experience the miracle of a deep breath.

Today, Higher Power, thank you for all the
miracles that happen every day.

Ever'thing there is but lovin'
leaves a rust on yo' soul.
—LANGSTON HUGHES

When I was active in my nicotine use, I did not know myself. I measured my self-worth with the opinions of others, and as a result despised myself. Nicotine helped me with that. My drug kept me in my "dis-ease," kept me from experiencing my true self and the world around me. For a long time, that was very comforting. But slowly, initially in another Twelve Step Program, I saw I could have more. I began to choose life and myself.

Nicotine Anonymous and the amazing people in the rooms became my Higher Power. From them I received unconditional love. With that secure base, I began, tentatively at first, to experience life without my drug. The amount of love and support I received encouraged me to try loving myself enough not to use nicotine.

Rust still lurks in the corners of my soul; I am still young in my recovery and always discovering something new about myself. But hour by hour, day by day, and through the love of this Program, I am cleaning my rust away and replacing it with trust.

Today, I will choose love and faith over fear and mistrust.

APRIL 6

"Keep Coming Back"
—TWELVE STEP SLOGAN

It was a miracle that I had been able to stop smoking through this Program. After being nicotine-free for three years, the meeting I traveled to sadly had to close. I continued to be free of nicotine for two more years with no meetings. Then it happened; I said, "I'll just have one." Within twenty-four hours I was smoking a pack.

I began to crawl back to this life-saving Program. It all began simply with the prayer, "please my Higher Power, I need help. Help me become willing to stop." Little by little it came, and once again I was granted the gift of being nicotine-free.

I belong to a group and it is a privilege to serve as a nicotine-free member. I love being a part of this beautiful Program. This is truly a gift, a gift that I choose not to return. I choose instead to treasure it and share it with others.

Praying for the willingness to quit nicotine was the humility I needed to let change seep into my life.

*Today, I ask for willingness and courage
in every difficult situation.*

You are in every moment
deciding who you are.
—NEALE DONALD WALSCH

Give or take a dozen, I attended a hundred and four Nicotine Anonymous meetings, basically two years' worth. I was not at all sure what I was doing there all that time. What I did know was that quitting my efforts to quit was not an option.

While I was attending meetings, I also turned my attention to creating a new lifestyle, one that did not include smoking. I began walking an hour each morning, doing an hour of posture exercises each afternoon and enrolled in a thrice-weekly exercise class. Another hour daily went into progressive relaxation and gratitude meditation. It was my hope that all this healthy living would, eventually, deaden the desire to do the opposite.

So many others had quit. Not one of those I had spoken with could tell me exactly why that last attempt was successful. This convinced me that, if I just kept trying, my turn too would come. It did.

Today, I will not give up on hope.

> It is good to have an end to journey toward; but it
> is the journey that matters in the end.
> —URSULA K. LE GUIN

S urrender. What makes it so hard to let go? I want so very much to
be in control. But the more I try to orchestrate everything, the more
it all slips from my grasp. My frustration at losing control makes me
want to sink back into my addiction.

I think having control is the answer. But when I really let go, when I
say, "take it God, it's yours" the clouds of frustration part. I finally
achieve the serenity I'm reaching for, sometimes just for a fleeting
moment. Ah, but such a blissful moment.

I cannot control life. I have to just let it happen.

---

*Today, I am willing "live life on life's
terms." That is how it has to be.*

I sought my soul, but my soul eluded me. I sought
my God, but my God I could not see. I sought my
brother and found all three.

—UNKNOWN

I had been trying unsuccessfully to quit using nicotine on my own for
over ten years. Hearing people share about how they were freed from
a seemingly hopeless enslavement to nicotine, a ray of hope parted
the thick clouds of my despair.

But my hope soon wilted.

After the initial relief of taking Step One, I hit a brick wall. A simple
three letter word, God, caused my mind to snap shut. If my success
depended upon the belief in a God, I was sunk. I might not be alive
today had it not been for the understanding group member who
proposed the following.

I was asked to picture myself home alone on my couch trying to stay
stopped by myself. I was asked to quantify, "how much power is in
that?" Next, I was asked to picture a fellowship of people with a
common problem, a common desire to solve their problem and a
common solution. "How much power is there in that?" "Is the unified
group a Power greater than me alone?"

I had to concede the obvious and with this fresh understanding of a
Power greater than me, the door to recovery swung open.

*Today, if I honestly do not and cannot believe in God, I will be
willing to be open for belief to develop. Willingness is the key.*

There is no higher religion than truth.

—MADAME BLAVADSKY

There are more warnings on a package of cigarettes than there are on a bottle of rat poison. I ignored them. To me these warnings were like the challenge to dash through a red light without getting a ticket. So what did finally get my attention?

"Truth" is my answer. I wanted to know how I really felt. Living in my addiction, every time I would recognize strong, uncomfortable feelings, I would medicate myself. When I lacked the courage to speak up, I would medicate myself. I was suffocating my thoughts, not just my lungs. I was peeking at my life through a drugged haze. Finally one day I said, "Okay God, I am ready for some more truth in my life." I wanted to know my own authentic heartbeat, not the pumped up, neurotic, apathetic point of view of my addiction. Nicotine was not just separating me from you; it was separating me from me.

My truth was by using nicotine, I was giving my spirit the messages of guilt, shame and fear because my spirit disagreed with the intake of this poison. Don't they pull people out of burning buildings for smoke inhalation? My first truth was I could drive without nicotine. This action brought me to another truth; I was here before nicotine. In order that I become free from nicotine, I had to stay in the truth all the time. If I medicated feelings how could I have intuitive guidance for and from myself? I started to get excited thinking about a life free from nicotine. I have been committed to service in Nicotine Anonymous for the past sixteen years, just to say thank you. That is my truth.

Today, I choose to know myself, to accept my feelings, and to listen to my inner guidance.

APRIL 11

Few are those who see with their own eyes and
feel with their own hearts.
—ALBERT EINSTEIN

Once I had a job as a receptionist and there was a surveillance monitor at my desk to display the view outside the front door. I would check the monitor whenever someone needed to be buzzed in, but the front stoop was where most of the smokers would sneak out for cigarettes. I think after a while, these people forgot they were on camera; it was almost as if I were spying on them.

When they were in groups, it was not as interesting. But when they were alone with their drug, the conflict in their expressions was clear. The nervous, darting eyes reminded me of how hard it was to shake off the guilt whenever I would light up. I used to put myself through that twenty or thirty times a day. By the time I had finished each cigarette, I would have convinced myself that everything was fine. My nicotine addiction and anything else troubling me were all just fine. I noticed the same resolve in those smokers' faces: the lips pursed in determination, the small self-assuring nods as they crushed out their cigarettes and went back to work.

They looked as if they were hitting a kind of reset button, and, I realized, that why I had smoked. Thankfully, after I put the cigarettes down and picked this Program up, I could see the reset button as a myth. There's nothing on this earth that can stop life or grant us any genuinely control over it. That can be a scary proposition, but most of the time it's been satisfying to live life on its own terms, honestly, unfiltered, and with no reset button.

Today, I am free to face life honestly. When I need support, I find it in Nicotine Anonymous and my Higher Power.

The more the marble is chipped away, the more
the statue grows.
—MICHELANGELO BUONARROTI

At a speakers meeting, the speaker told of her release from the craving to smoke. "After about eight weeks, I woke up one morning and realized just how good I felt. A wave of gratitude came in. Since then I have felt the gratitude, and not the urge to smoke. I never believed that I would be able to not smoke for so long." I am happy to tell you that it is weeks since that meeting and she is still free of nicotine.

Each of us experiences getting free in a different way. Each time I had quit in the past, the experience was different. What does it matter? Just getting free at all is such a wonder. Why compare? If it makes my day lighter and easier to hear how a fellow nicotine addict succeeded, then I get to all the meetings I can find. I let the sharing give me courage and comfort and hope.

If my mood is low, I may be tempted to miss the point of listening to others sharing at a meetings. A story of success may feel like a reminder of my failure. Or, when another member tells of losing the urge to smoke, I might want to run right out and light up.

*Today, I remember that addiction and a low mood
can twist everything. This usually happens just
when I most need to listen with an open mind.*

That's why I've come to you, to seek release from
a curse of misery and horror against which I'm
powerless to fight alone.

—"COUNT DRACULA," BRAM STOKER

I believed that smoking was a reward. A bad day at work, a disagreement with my spouse, or a boring activity provided me with all the reasons I needed to smoke. I made nicotine my reward for putting up with the unpleasant parts of life. In reality, I was addicted so I was clever enough to create reasons for reaching for another nicotine fix.

By making the decision to turn my will and life over to the care and will of God I am choosing life and health over a false reward that can only destroy me. The ability to choose to turn my life and will over is all the reward I could want. No problem is too big, no task too unpleasant, and no sadness too great for God. All I have to do is turn them over and reap the benefits of my choice.

Today, I celebrate my ability to turn my life and will over to God. God's will is my reward.

Let the pain push you until the vision pulls you.
—DR. MICHAEL BECKWITH

After making it through a particularly rough day, I remember catching myself thinking, "I deserve a reward." Before I knew what hit me, I had justified going out into a cold, rainy night to a liquor store that sold cigarettes, two for a quarter. Another several week period of abstinence from nicotine went up in smoke.

Following the familiar hangover of self-disgust, something happened. I burst out laughing. It struck me, the absurdity of it all. I had successfully deluded and convinced myself that I deserved to inhale poison. I had crazily crafted a nicotine (and cancer) delivery system into a reward.

Was this a loving way to treat myself, someone I supposedly loved? What were the sane and healthy choices? How about a fruit smoothie or a stick of sugarless gum or a hot bath? Once I began exploring, I found a whole menu of possible options. In fact, I wrote down twenty and carried the piece of paper in my wallet. Whenever a craving hit, I pulled out my menu and would invariably find the best choice for that moment. For many years now, that choice has been many things other than nicotine in any form.

Addiction is said to be a disease of perception. We can develop a confusion of needs. We can come to think we need things that we really don't need. We can come to think that we don't need things that we really do need.

*Today, I can tell the difference between a
reward and a self-destructive lie.*

Are these extravagant promises? We think not. They are being fulfilled among us—sometimes quickly, sometimes slowly. They will always materialize if we work for them.

—ALCOHOLICS ANONYMOUS

After many unsuccessful and demoralizing attempts to stay stopped from my addiction, I was led to Nicotine Anonymous. The first word I heard was, "welcome." I was surprised to continually feel welcomed even though I could not seem to stay clean. Several times I almost talked myself into quitting the Program since I could not quit feeding my addiction. I felt ashamed to collect still another newcomer chip. But at the end of each meeting I heard the encouraging words, "keep coming back."

Not just the words but the genuine sentiment of "welcome" and "keep coming back" kept me in the boat, kept me in position for the power of the Fellowship and the power of the Program of Nicotine Anonymous to overpower my obsession to use nicotine.

One day in the spring of 1993, I realized that I had gone the whole week in between my Friday night Step Study meeting without even thinking about using. The obsession had been removed. I was free.

If I feel discouraged by apparent setbacks or imperfections, I look around the room at a meeting, I see people who did not stay stopped from their first meeting. But they stayed in the boat and now some are three weeks, three months or three years free.

Today, I am willing to surrender to the process; to trust and to "keep coming back," no matter what happens.

God spares our weakness, by only showing us our
own deformity by degree, and as He gives us
strength to bear the sight.

—ARCHBISHOP FRANCOIS FENELON

D oes smoking help people accomplish more? Or, is a smoker a
lazy person who "sits on his butt and puffs away"? I always
thought I did more as a smoker, but today I started to see a big
truth in the other point of view.

When I thought of quitting smoking, I feared losing my ability to
hurry, my hustle-bustle image. It is true, I did lose some nervous energy
when I quit. Sometimes now I miss the jolt to my system from the
nicotine, but then I have also cut back on caffeine. Was my nervous
energy productive? I think I only ran in circles faster. I do not think I
actually accomplished more. And I sometimes pushed myself when I was
already exhausted, using the combination of nicotine and caffeine, and
diet pills too at one time in my life.

I became aware of the other side of the issue about smoking and
activity. I discovered that I have some lazy times built into my routine. I
certainly approve of rest, relaxation, and some idle time. Looking at this
honestly, I had to admit that I have allowed myself excessive idle time.
Smoking used to give me the idea that I was doing something. I was busy
having a cigarette. I was also reading or watching TV, but don't ask me to
tell you what the show or book was about. I know today that I was not
refreshed by that type of relaxing.

---

*Today, I choose to enjoy my lazy time. I will consider if I
can relax with a clear conscience, or if I am running
away from something I should be doing.*

APRIL 17

This too shall pass.

—JESUS OF NAZARETH

I just realized that I had been unconsciously nibbling on my thumbnail. How many times I was accused of getting oral gratification through my nicotine habit. When I had tried to stop using in the past, I had always gained weight. "Proof that they were right," I would think. "I am seeking oral gratification."

The idea of oral gratification implies an infant wanting to nurse. The comment was a judgment that my behavior was immature and motivated by unresolved forces from my infancy. I resented non-smokers for pointing out my weakness. If possible, I would take a cigarette out of the pack and light up, as though that cigarette would lift my lowered sense of myself. I assumed that my pursed lips and resentment were hidden by the nasty stream of smoke I blew out.

I will probably never know enough about my early days of life to understand why I crave oral gratification. Does it matter? Can I survive without satisfying the urge? Obviously I can. For six seconds the urge oppresses me. I almost believe that I cannot go on without using. I can prove how silly that fear is by recalling the times when I could refrain, even though I felt overwhelmed by the urge.

Today, I know that many things trigger cravings and relaxing with a deep breath or repeating a slogan or the Serenity Prayer will help me cope.

We begin to have a fuller understanding of the
meaning of our lives, and function better in our
daily activities and relationships.

—NICOTINE ANONYMOUS MEMBER

One of our Nicotine Anonymous members celebrated his first
nicotine-free year of his adult life. The cake and card from the
group were fun. We were proud to let him know how much we
admired his accomplishment. His smile was the happiest, proudest smile
I have seen in a long time.

In a way, each of us there celebrated our own victory too: six weeks
for one, four months for another, forty-eight precious hours for another.
These are hardcore addicts who found a way to get free and stay free of
nicotine, with the help of the Program. The gentle feeling of gratitude
brushes by our minds.

I believe that each person in the group has a special understanding
and acceptance of the other group members. I see a caring and a concern
about the struggles, problems, and growth that each member experiences.
And that special night I saw each member proud as can be of our hero,
our member with a whole year free of nicotine.

Our group discussed whether recovery is the same as not using. Our
one year member is a great example of the difference. He comes to
meetings. He actively sponsors many others, but it took a little time to
open up emotionally and spiritually. At that point he began his recovery.
He gives us all hope and strength.

*Today, I remember what other Twelve Step Programs
say, "He came. He came to. He came to believe."*

The courage to change the things we can.

—REINHOLD NIEBUHR

Nicotine is my friend. When I stop using, I get depressed. I feel like I am losing my best friend. When I became addicted to nicotine, I told myself this lie to protect my habit.

One of the signs of addiction is "stinking thinking." This harsh little phrase is a good label for the twisted logic I can use to deny my problem. Honest thinking will tell me that the drug nicotine is no friend. As I struggle for air, I know that painful, life-threatening disease is the work of a bitter enemy, not a friend.

In the past I quit using many times, only to eventually cave in, lying to myself that just one would be okay. Months or years later I would remember that I had meant to stay off tobacco. Where did I lose sight of the goal? It is uncomfortable to unmask the lies I have lived with for years. If I can truly change my thinking to accept that nicotine is an insidious, deadly addiction, I will be better able to catch myself when my thinking gets distorted.

Today, I will remember the mythical sirens who lured sailors to their deaths by singing irresistible songs. I will no longer create my own siren's songs.

Go and learn how to unlearn.
—CHARLES PEGUY

Maturity is defined as the ability to withstand trials without breaking, and triumphs without losing oneself. With wry humor, I may find myself an expert in the withstanding trials category. Life does have its share of lumps. Let me take a minute to think about a few ways that I may be reacting when I face a problem.

Sometimes I may react to a setback by wallowing in self-pity. Did you ever hear the old saying that "self-pity is like a dirty diaper: at first it is warm and comfortable, but after a while it stinks"? Self-pity can warp character and diminish my dignity. Did I settle into a favorite chair, puff up a thick haze of smoke, and wallow in my sadness? Now without the cigarette, it is easier to see the line between feeling hurt and dragging it over into self-pity.

Another reaction to troubles is also common. I can pretend to be untouched by the problem. Using used to be a good way to pretend I did not notice, didn't it? The danger to me is that this false pose hampers the healthy expression of my humanity. As I continue this charade, I deaden my connection with my very self.

Today, there is a fresh breeze blowing through my life: energy surges through me; breathing is less labored; emotions become unblocked. "Just for today" I feel brand-new.

A thought which does not result in an action is
nothing much, and an action which does not
proceed from a thought is nothing at all.

—GEORGES BERNANOS

Have you ever noticed someone at a party juggling a drink and a small plate of food in one hand, while smoking a cigarette with the other hand? The saying, "There but for the grace of God go I" pops into mind. I remember the juggling act with food, drink, and smoke to hide my nervousness at social events. I always had a spare pack with me, because I knew I could not stay and socialize if I ran out of cigarettes.

When I thought of giving up smoking, I felt an overwhelming dread of being with other people without my crutch. Smoking had provided me with something to do when I felt anxious. Would I become awkward? Could I cope with emotions from an uncomfortable situation or an embarrassing remark?

In some ways my addicted self was smarter than my thinking now. When I smoked, I planned ahead so that my nicotine supply would be secure. If I am projecting feelings of fear into situations that have not occurred yet, I can think smarter. I can plan ways to get through a trying situation as comfortably as possible. I can wear a piece of jewelry for my hands to fidget with as I chat. I can plan to look for healthful foods to nibble on, to maintain my weight. I can plan on asking for non-alcoholic drinks to avoid weakening my resolve in this pressured situation. Alcohol triggers my nicotine addiction. With several helpful ideas in mind, I can begin to anticipate the event with confidence.

Today, I will savor the victory of getting through a challenge successfully. What a satisfying and proud feeling it is to handle a difficult situation well.

The battle, sir, is not to the strong
alone; it is to the vigilant.
—PATRICK HENRY

Some members enjoy subtle changes in their relationships. Their loved ones are more eager to hug and kiss them now that they do not reek of tobacco. Other members tell of feeling more confident when they are physically close to other people. A few of them even hear words of praise and encouragement for quitting.

It is important that my mind is perfectly clear. I have quit for myself. It is very satisfying to hear praise for my efforts, but I cannot depend on receiving praise, understanding or support. It is also possible to get criticized for a temporary weight gain, for irritability, or for other things that have nothing to do with quitting. Is criticism a good reason to feed my addiction?

Nicotine Anonymous is a selfish Program. It teaches me that I must place my freedom from nicotine as my first priority. Even if I stopped for someone else, my recovery depends on taking responsibility for the decision to stay quit. I find pleasure in compliments and praise, but those words only add to my inner satisfaction.

When the winds of opinion push me one way and another, I can temporarily lose my sense of direction. What a good time to reach out to my sponsor or to read a piece of literature. When things calm down, I will feel great peace inside for weathering the storm with my goals intact. The Program can be a wonderful rudder to keep me headed toward my goal, freedom from my nicotine addiction.

Today, I will stay focused on my goal.
No distraction can pull me off course.

The grand essentials of happiness are: something to do,
something to love, and something to hope for.
—ALLAN K. CHALMERS

I wake up this morning and I have a beautiful new day ahead of me.
My morning routines are not dulled by a foggy head from
yesterday's nicotine. I wash and dress, happy that I will not be
fouling my clothes or body. I enjoy my breakfast. If coffee triggers
longings for nicotine, I will drink juice or tea.

I can choose to make today a happy day. I can look for ways to add
enjoyment to my schedule. I can be alert to a lovely view on my way to
my day's appointments. I can savor a delicious taste. I think of people
who uplift me, and I promise myself the gift of talking with such a
person today.

I can walk today without losing my breath. Just for the pleasure of it,
I will do some physical exercise today that is more of a challenge than
usual. This day without nicotine has all kinds of new possibilities. As I
gain strength in the Program, I find that I can reach out to someone who
may need an encouraging word. I find joy in being able to help someone
else.

*Today, I will make this day the kind of day I want it to
be. Not everything in this day will be to my liking, but I
will choose how I will react. When the day is over, I will
think back on this day with pleasure.*

Success is a science; if you have the
conditions, you get the result.
—OSCAR WILDE

When I struggle to free myself from my addiction to nicotine, I start a wonderful journey. My first steps are hesitant and difficult, while I wrestle with the drug still in my body. As that subsides, I start tripping over the habit and the things that remind me, things that trigger the urge to smoke.

I gain some confidence as the urges become less frequent. Am I ready to graduate from Nicotine Anonymous? I find that this is a tricky time. While I am nicotine-free with ease now for much of the time, there is danger here. Challenging situations may stir up emotions that seem to overwhelm me. Like a cleverly built tiger pit trap, I can fall right into my old solution, nicotine. What can nicotine do to change the situation? It can only add another problem to my difficulties.

Applying the Program during such trials is working the Program. It is difficult work to revamp the patterns I have lived by. I do not have to travel the journey on my own. I have a Higher Power to depend on when the road is too hard. This Power is stronger than me, or any of us, alone. It will carry me through the most trying times. I know that my nicotine addiction is physical, emotional, and spiritual in its impact.

*Today, with the help of my group, my sponsor and my Higher
Power, I have the tools to build a satisfying life, free of nicotine.*

We shall pay any price, bear any burden, meet any
hardship, support any friend, oppose any foe to
assure the survival and the success of liberty.
—JOHN F. KENNEDY

I am embarrassed at feeling so out of control. I want to cry, scream, pound on walls. I feel wrenching sobs deep inside that I cannot release. The old answer was to use nicotine, and last night I did. I had a slip. A difficult problem was my excuse last night. Today I still have the problem, but now I have nicotine cravings too. Now I see the insanity in what I have done. Should I laugh or cry?

How lucky I am that someone from the Program called me a few minutes ago. I had been toying with the idea of just continuing to live in my addiction. The temptation feels overwhelming, just like when I first stopped. No. Getting free from nicotine must be my number one priority. That other problem will just have to take a back seat right now. I must get through these cravings. That will take all my concentration right now.

What can I do to strengthen my recovery? Why was I so vulnerable when this problem surfaced? I realize that I have lost focus on my Program lately. A variety of things can cause me to drift away from working the Program. Each time I let some excuse wedge itself between me and my recovery, I run a great danger of slipping back into addiction. I know it is important for me to read Program literature daily. I need to talk with Program people regularly. I must go to Nicotine Anonymous meetings. I had gotten complacent about my recovery.

*Today, I remember that nothing is more
precious to me than my recovery.*

Speak clearly, if you speak at all;
carve every word before you let it fall.
—OLIVER WENDELL HOLMES

When I was using, I resented the holier-than-thou attitude of non-smokers. I promised myself that I would never be like that when I gave up cigarettes. Now I am having second thoughts about what is right.

As a nicotine addict, I resented anyone who would not go along with my smoking. I wanted others to act as enablers, allowing me to be comfortable with my habit. To be honest, I was nasty when someone challenged me. I would be sarcastic one time, indignant at another time, hoping to intimidate the person into going along with my smoking request.

It takes tough love to say no to someone who wants change for the cigarette machine, or who asks to light up in a small room. How well I know their annoyance if I refuse. Can I gracefully put aside the request? If I stop enabling, this person might face his nicotine addiction. If I refuse in a way that stirs up anger, I am probably handing him another excuse to avoid looking at his addiction. When I am firm and clear about my rights to a smoke-free environment, I am strengthening my Program. I am also improving my health. Inhaling the nicotine in secondary smoke is a real risk for me.

Today, I will set and enforce boundaries that allow me to continue my recovery, but I will do so as graciously as I can.

An error doesn't become a mistake
until you refuse to correct it.
—ORLANDO A. BATTISTA

A member told a moving story at our meeting. She had quit smoking for six years, but now was hooked into her old habit again. How had it happened? At the funeral of her twin sister, someone had offered her a cigarette in a misguided attempt to console her. Now, three years later, she was still smoking. What a vicious, unrelenting thing this addiction is. How cruel to attack when we lack our usual strength. Does this mean that I am doomed to relapse into nicotine addiction? No, a million times no.

There is hope. I have others to care for me, hear my sorrows, wishes, failures and dreams. I have meetings to attend, literature to read. Certainly people quit smoking without attending meetings or trying to improve their emotional and spiritual lives through a Program. They just quit. And some even stay quit the rest of their lives.

Then why do I leave my warm house on a cold, wet night to get to a meeting? I find people at my meetings who listen to me. I meet people who understand my struggles as only another nicotine addict can. I get new insight and inspiration to improve my life and grow. When a dreary day makes me feel too weary to go to a meeting, let me remember the benefits I gain from going. How often I have heard just the right word to help me with a situation. And there have surely been times where my story has meant something special to another person there.

*Today, I will absorb the wisdom of others,
and allow others to share my experience.*

Good friends are good for your health.

—DR. IRWIN SARASON

For me, it might be a good test of my emotional recovery to see if I can find something to laugh about in a day, not a sarcastic laugh, but a warm and loving, accepting laugh. I can get caught up in very serious concerns, full of stormy emotions. What a blessing to all around me if I can just back off. A Twelve Step Program is supposed to deflate my overblown ego, and that is just what I need. Spare me from my almighty opinion.

With the gentle guidance of friends in the Program, I can learn to sort out where my ego is getting me in trouble, and where I must firmly speak my truth. Sometimes the simple act of accepting me, with the warmth and caring that I feel from my Nicotine Anonymous friends, gives me the strength to catch myself and do better. The quiet acceptance of the others in my group can be a powerful medicine to heal my pains and hurts. Their understanding of my addictive behavior can help me head off a relapse into smoking, and bolster my newfound maturity.

Today, I am grateful for laughter
and my growing maturity.

To rejoice in another person's joy
is like being in heaven.
—MEISTER ECKHART

Smoking is a constricting noose. It shuts down my lungs, and it closes down my contact with the world. Do you doubt what I'm saying? I watch a new member open up, grow, and blossom before my own eyes, and I realize how far I have come. I have seen the miracle happen.

Each of us progresses at a different pace, of course. There is no timetable. Each moves to a hidden dance, a personal rhythm. There are times when I know I have grown. New attitudes, new patterns for living spring into my life. Then I have times when nothing seems to change for the longest time.

One member reports with pride that she has stopped coughing when she gets up in the morning. I notice how relaxed her face is. Her face has become animated. Before, her face was deadpan. Now I see a lively person expressing feelings and life. I see my own recovery reflected in the faces around me.

Today, I see my progress mirrored in the faces of my friends in the Program, and I give thanks for their companionship.

Whatever you can do or dream, begin it. Boldness
has genius, power and magic in it. Begin it now!
—JOHANN WOLFGANG VON GOETHE

There is an urge in me to grow. One way it is showing itself is that I am giving up nicotine. This same urge to grow has led me to the Fellowship of others in Nicotine Anonymous. Many doors to a new life will open for me now.

I have struggled to get past the early stages of withdrawal from the addiction. My focus is not limited to giving up nicotine anymore. My focus is shifting to accepting a fuller and richer life. I have opened my days to involvement with others. I do not run away when emotions gets awkward. I may be uncomfortable experiencing such closeness, but I survive it. Survive? That squirming and fidgeting from a sweet closeness with a friend is a happy problem and a joy. I did not know the flavors that friendship offers when I used nicotine to avoid intimacy.

I tolerate the feelings I feel more vividly now, both the happy and the painful ones. Yes, nicotine dulled pain. But that was merely burying the pain to experience it more honestly someday in the future. When I put the cigarettes away, those feelings came forward from the storehouse of my heart, and the first few months of facing those feelings were emotionally exhausting indeed.

Once the flood of emotions becomes manageable, I find that life is a richer and swifter flowing stream. I discover I can handle rough times. Time changes things. Soon I find myself floating in moments of serenity.

*Today, without nicotine, I experience
life in all its wonder.*

It is tragic how few people ever possess their souls before
they die. Their thoughts are someone else's opinions, their
lives a mimicry, their passions a quotation.

—OSCAR WILDE

Where do I put my energy? Do I direct my focus to the good and the positive? Is my mind allowed to run wild? Do I guide my thinking to the green pastures where they belong? I find that I have a tendency to follow negative thought patterns, projecting terrible problems, harboring resentment, holding grudges, and pitying myself. Did I stop growing the day I started using nicotine?

There is room for improvement in my habits of mind. If I ever start to list the failings of my loved ones, let me quickly remember my own imperfection. I am responsible for myself. I cannot control or change any other person. When I am tempted to begin inspecting another's life for faults, let me pick up a mirror first and examine my own. As I finish identifying and correcting all my own failings, then I am qualified to control myself.

When I look at my failings, it requires a mature honesty to also remember my good and strong qualities. It is my good and strong qualities that become the foundation for all lasting improvement that I can achieve.

*Today, I will take only my own
inventory. That's quite enough.*

Man's mind once stretched by a new idea, never
regains its original dimension.
—OLIVER WENDELL HOLMES

Sometimes I was so desperate for a nicotine fix that I would pick up a
cigarette butt from the sidewalk when I did not have enough money
to buy them. This is behavior characteristic of a true addict. But I
never viewed myself as an addict. I was a smoker. Our society views
smokers as people who engage in a nasty, filthy habit. This is no mere
habit though, as I have discovered when I tried to stop for even one day.

Nicotine is as powerful a drug as any, if not more powerful. Society
acts in an enabling role, making this drug legal, but just because it is legal
does not mean that the nicotine addict will escape its gripping effect. I
have stopped, but I need to reaffirm on a daily basis my powerlessness
over this deadly chemical. For me, there is no such thing as just one. I
cannot risk becoming complacent. With the help of my Higher Power, I
will not give in to the temporary urge that may sometimes come over me.

*Today, I will remember that I am a nicotine addict. I may have a
craving, but I will not answer the craving with nicotine.*

Too often we underestimate the power of a touch,
a smile, a kind word, a listening ear, an honest
compliment, or the smallest act of caring, all of
which have the potential to turn a life around.

—LEO BUSCAGLIA

Nicotine addiction is becoming a worldwide problem. At home I am only part of one small Nicotine Anonymous group, but my heart dreams of the day when Nicotine Anonymous is available to every nicotine addict, no matter what country or language.

In the United States, the Surgeon General has ordered that a warning be printed on every pack of cigarettes. As a smoker, I noticed the health warning, but what I read did not register. Somehow I felt immune to the harmful effects of tobacco. The coughing, shortness of breath, and irritability seemed normal. They certainly had nothing to do with my smoking.

The denial associated with nicotine addiction is very elusive. When I am in the grip of denial, I believe lies. Now, it boggles my mind how I ever believed some of the lies. How grateful I am that I can live with the truth. The truth is that I am powerless over nicotine. This truth bridges every barrier of culture or language to lovingly enfold us all.

When I am in a moment of weakness, I can check my thoughts and turn to a Power greater than myself for relief from this insane thinking, whether through prayer, attending a Nicotine Anonymous meeting, or by calling a fellow non-using nicotine addict.

Today, "one day at a time," one hour at a time, or one minute at a time I can practice living my life as a healing non-smoker proudly regaining my health in many ways.

... The wisdom to know the difference.

—REINHOLD NIEBUHR

In frustration with the concepts of powerlessness and the Higher Power, a member called an old friend for guidance. "Think of it this way," he was told. "You are powerless over nicotine. You prove it to yourself every time you leave the house in the middle of the night because you are out of cigarettes. And there are dozens of other examples. Tell me are you in control then, or is nicotine?"

The other question was answered as simply: "A Higher Power is anything that is stronger than nicotine. Do you believe that there is any force stronger than nicotine?"

It has often been said that this is a simple Program for complicated people. I have made life unnaturally complex with my addict's twisted logic. In Nicotine Anonymous I am given simple principles to guide me and simple slogans to get me through my confusion. The trick is to live them outside of the meeting rooms. That takes effort. I must work to recall these concepts when I am at a low point, and I must fight years of behaving one way to try this new and healthier way of behaving. That is very hard work indeed. This is where I truly have power, in the ability to change myself. The concerns outside me are usually beyond my ability to control.

Today, I will concentrate on applying one slogan or one concept of the Program, just to practice changing and growing.

> If we really understand the problem, the answer
> will come out of it because the answer is not
> separate from the problem.
> —JIDDU KRISHNAMURTI

D id you ever watch a child in a store, resisting and struggling with a grown-up? What a lot of energy the child spends digging in his heels and fighting the inevitable. Eventually the little one resumes the shopping trip and harmony is restored.

The years may or may not make me wiser. Do I have a problem at work or at home that is draining the energy out of me? Let me look at my own part, only myself, in this situation for a moment. Is my energy going into resisting, fighting facts, avoiding dealing with something I would rather not accept?

It is not the loss of a battle to adopt an attitude of acceptance. Acceptance does not mean giving in to unacceptable things. Acceptance simply means acknowledging reality. Once I stop fighting it and accept the painful reality, then I am free to decide what I must do as a mature person.

I feel that it is a mark of my progress that I can usually get a hurtful reality through my thick skull in a few days now. I can think of similar problems where it took weeks or months for me to hear what people were trying to tell me. And on some issues I never have heard.

Today, I will accept each problem and find the answer.

If you think you're too small to have an impact, try
going to bed with a mosquito in the room.

—ANITA RODDICK

When I am coping with nicotine withdrawal, I may not be able to cope with the people close to me in my life. I may lose perspective and view them as being the cause of my unhappiness. I am angry. I may say hurtful things.

This is a good time to practice detaching. At first, the most basic way to detach is to get out of the room or to go outside for a walk. Let the steam off elsewhere. Less harm is done this way.

In time I may learn to stay in the room, but detach from the words or actions that set me off. One mother pretends to put cotton in her ears to stop hearing the kids bickering. By staying serene, she discovered that she now could help. Before, she used to become involved; she was a part of the problem. Another acts as if his partner deserved courtesy and kindness when the partner seemed to deserve anything but kindness. He found that the partner responded to this treatment, improving his attitude and behavior in just a little while.

If all I can do is to detach physically, that is good. It is so much better than staying in the situation and causing hurt. Nothing is gained by fooling myself on this point.

Today, I will remember to practice detachment.

I have learnt silence from the talkative, toleration from
the intolerant, and kindness from the unkind; yet
strange, I am ungrateful to these teachers.

—KAHLIL GIBRAN

Well, what a surprise. I just realized that I did not think once about wanting a cigarette this whole day. I am feeling pleased with myself.

True, I did notice that a person near me smoked. A few times I became aware of it. Once I noted clouds of smoke rising to the ceiling in the office. What of it? What is that to me? Nothing. I saw people lighting cigarettes. One even clutched a cigarette until he was outside and could legally light it. I did not long to be one of the smokers today. I did not get too smug either. It was like a leaf fell off a tree, I saw it, but it meant nothing to me.

The people I work with do not know that I ever smoked. I started this new job about a month after I quit. I smile to think that they assume that I am a non-smoker. After being an addict who smoked over 250,000 cigarettes, I feel thrilled that anyone might assume that I never smoked.

I am free from wasting any of my energy, time, health or mental powers on smoking. I am on a victorious journey. Every day is another positive step along the way. Whenever I forget to be grateful or take for granted my new status, I get in some type of emotional pain.

Today, I will stop frequently to feel grateful.

God, help me to victory over myself, for difficult
to conquer is oneself, though when that is
conquered, all is conquered.

—JAIN PRAYER

As we come in the doors of our Nicotine Anonymous meetings, we bring attitudes with us that are special to each of us, our own personal issues. Steady attendance at meetings, application of the Steps and Traditions will open the path for me. I will understand the message of the Program as it best fits my individual needs.

People who are new to the Steps usually resist the ideas of powerlessness over nicotine. For many, the concept of a Higher Power raises objections, often related to the God of their childhood. For me personally, the term insanity provokes fear. I am troubled by the word as I study the Steps.

I came into Nicotine Anonymous with years of exposure to the Steps through other Programs, and the challenge for me is to balance priorities correctly. Giving up nicotine will cause personal upheaval. As a dual-Program person, I must honestly consider the strength of my other Program in the light of nicotine withdrawal. The guidance of a knowing and loving sponsor may be critical to my success.

Is it possible to give up nicotine without the Steps? Of course. Is it better to outgrow my addicted mentality to a better way of life?

Today, I will work the Program.
Growth is important.

The only tyrant I accept is the
still small voice within me.
—MAHATMA GANDHI

After I have put aside nicotine for a while, the physical withdrawal symptoms are mostly gone. At moments I see how my health returns. I feel happy inside. I have talked at meetings about handling life without my stage prop. I make progress with my feelings, and start to feel more comfortable with people, even without nicotine.

What spiritual thread is constant through all these changes? What practical philosophy gives me direction? Again and again I hear members acknowledge that their answers were always there within themselves. I may clear my thinking by talking things through with a sponsor. In peace and quietness, I may hear my own wisest counsel. If I listen honestly to my own guidance, I will know what is right for me.

Sometimes my mind is too absorbed in people or events. When I lose touch with my sense of myself, I get tripped up in envy, frustration, hurt, self-pity, despair or hate. I am far from centered in what is good and strong in me. I give my serenity away too cheaply.

Today, I will study myself to become a better person. As I am able to express myself in healthier ways, I make my little corner of the world a better place.

Look to this day, for it is life, the very life of life
... the glory of power for yesterday is but a dream
and tomorrow is only a vision. But today, well
lived, makes every yesterday a dream of happiness
and every tomorrow a vision of hope.
—MAHAKAVI KALIDASA

"One day at a time," one minute at a time, and one decision at a time was the key to making my first twenty-four hours. When I came to Nicotine Anonymous, I had exhausted all my resources to get free of nicotine. I had been to another Twelve Step Program and tried "let go and let God," the Sixth and Seventh Steps, remove these character defects, the Eleventh Step but I always returned to nicotine.

I needed the recovering Nicotine Addict. Finally, I asked a friend to help me start a Nicotine Anonymous group. He agreed instantly. We held meetings and he said, "just take it one day at a time; be nice to yourself because you are so fragile right now."

I think when I read *Nicotine Anonymous—The Book* it was instant hope, and that load I had been carrying on my shoulder was gone. I was no longer alone. I believe having just one minute, one decision, one day at time was my key. Talking to other nicotine addicts about my struggle made it so much easier. They knew exactly how I felt and what I was going through. One day they said, "sound likes fear to me." I had not known what this big load was. They got me through that day.

If I have one foot in yesterday and one foot in tomorrow then I am messing up today. Living in the now and "just for today" are some good tools. Every morning I read the Third Step Prayer.

Today, I will keep both feet solidly in the present.

I don't know what the future holds,
but I know Who holds it."
—BILLY GRAHAM

How was I supposed to get through that night? A single parent described a night of fear when her only child flew on a five-hour trip. This mother discovered that she had smoked a whole pack of cigarettes while she waited for the call that all was okay.

We use the term projecting to describe a habit of mind that feeds worry. When I project, I usually imagine very painful events. For some reason I give these thoughts substance and dwell on them until this fit of worry passes. When I am free of its grip, I easily see the error of assuming only the worst.

When I am upset, I cannot just stop thinking. Luckily, I cannot think of two things at the same time. I use my mental powers wisely. I can plan how to deal with the things that concern me. I concentrate on the most realistic outcomes and plan how I will handle them.

What else can I do when I am tense with worry? I can try to relax, live the next five minutes the best I can, right where I am. As the saying recommends, "If you're doing the dishes, let your mind be where your hands are."

*Today, I can calm down, relax, and get
in a more reasonable frame of mind.*

We admitted we were powerless over nicotine,
that our lives had become unmanageable.
—STEP ONE

Before I took this Step, nicotine was my master. Being powerless, my life revolved around the consumption of nicotine. I responded to the craving's call whenever it wanted me to. What aspects of my life were affected by this unmanageability? My health, environment, repressed feelings, finances, relationships with other people.... This list sometimes seems endless.

Taking this Step for the first time, I felt defeated, boxed in. I felt as though I could not stop. I was trapped by this insidious chemical called nicotine. I had tried to stop hundreds of times before, but always failed. I could sink no lower. Somehow this time seemed worse than the others. I had hit a bottom of my addiction. I could no longer believe the denial. I was reminded that some people hit their bottom only when they die.

After I took Step One, I was ready to take the next Step. I made the frightening decision to stop using nicotine. I felt at peace with myself and with my decision to stop using. I also felt uncomfortable. Why would this be different from the many other times I have stopped? That was when I begin to look for help to stop and to stay stopped.

Today, I freely admit I am powerless over nicotine. If the thought of feeding my addiction becomes attractive, I will stop and remind myself of the unmanageability of fueling my addiction.

Came to believe that a Power greater than
ourselves could restore us to sanity.
—STEP TWO

Before I took this Step, I often tried to stay stopped as I did in the past. I tried to do it my way. But from experience, I realized that I could not do it alone.

With this Step, I reached out for help. The Power greater than myself is often the love and support in a Nicotine Anonymous meeting. I saw the Nicotine Anonymous Program as a sanction for my battered lungs, defeated spirit and confused mind. I saw that Power as my unique definition of a Divine spirit or being.

Sanity means soundness or health of mind. A good example of this is the acknowledgment of my denial and my refusal to believe it now that I have a desire to recover. After taking this Step, I hear recovering Nicotine Anonymous members share their "experience, strength and hope" and see that there is a way to stop, stay stopped and be at peace with my decision.

Today, I will acknowledge the Power greater than myself, be it a Nicotine Anonymous meeting, a prayer to a Higher Power, or contacting a recovering nicotine addict.

Everything in life that we really
accept undergoes a change.

—KATHERINE MANSFIELD

I was in the hospital with a lung disease, and I still found myself sneaking into a nurse's pocketbook to steal a cigarette. I could not get my breath one morning as I got out of bed. I ran out into the snow, with only my underwear on, to shock my system into breathing again. Still I did not quit. What have I sacrificed for this addiction?

Step One puts the situation out in the open: I admitted I was powerless. If the addiction did not have me trapped in its grip, I would not have gone back a thousand times after saying, "I've had it. I'm not going to let this happen to me." I know I am powerless when I watch my firm resolve melt into nothing.

One of the members of my group said she got used to smoking tape. I asked her why. She told about the many times she had broken her cigarettes in half, only to come back to the garbage can an hour later to fish out the biggest pieces to mend with tape, and then smoke. I laughed, but I had done some pretty silly things too.

I can now surrender to my Higher Power to guide me and lead me into right actions that will remove the obsession with smoking and the addiction to the drug nicotine. Admitting that I am powerless brings the relief of courageously facing the truth. The struggle to control the addiction is over at last.

*Today, I will surrender my life and my
will to the care of my Higher Power.*

To forgive is to set the prisoner free, and then
discover the prisoner was you.
—LEWIS SMEDES

One day when I was sixteen, my father brutally beat me. Until that day, I had been spared the physical abuse my siblings suffered. I was the good one, the one who kept the others out of trouble, or at least tried to make sure they did not get caught.

That beating killed any feeling of love I had for my father. I had little to say to him. I did not want to be in the same room with him.

Since I came into the Program, I have prayed to be relieved of that resentment. And, I have prayed to be able to see my part in the disagreement that preceded the beating. All I could see was that for once I stuck up for myself instead of keeping peace at any price. Gradually over the past few years I began to see my father as a flawed human rather than as a monster. But I still could not open my heart to him. Then some friends had a serious disagreement with other mutual friends and left our circle. I found myself asking them if one action could justify throwing away all the good from the relationship. I realized I had found my own answer.

My part was in refusing to love or be loved for over thirty-five years. Now I can see that his few minutes of rage was small compared to my years of distance. Without question, my wrong was vastly greater than his. Fortunately I saw the truth in time to make amends before he died.

*Today, God help me stay focused on only my part
and replace resentment with forgiveness and love.*

Came, Came To, Came to Believe
—ALCOHOLICS ANONYMOUS

I am a physician. I had seen emphysema patients plug up their tracheotomy tubes so they could smoke. I saw my father die from emphysema. I carefully followed research on the consequences of using nicotine. Twice I spent $1,000 for inpatient stop-smoking programs. I tried hypnosis and other programs. I could have run a stop-smoking seminar.

But the knowledge did me no good. Always my emotions got the best of me. I blew up, and I smoked at the person, place or event.

I knew I was slowly killing myself. I had become so despondent, I had smoked more. The only commitment I could make would be to buy only one pack at a time, preserving the slender thread of hope that I might stop sometime and not have to waste the rest of the carton. Many times I left behind half-empty packs, but I would check the location each hour to see if someone had taken the gift.

Then I found Nicotine Anonymous. I learned to "let go and let God."

Thank you God, for doing for me what I cannot do for myself.

Today, I can truly experience life. Today, challenges don't trigger a reflex to smoke. Today, I can share my "experience, strength and hope" with another who still struggles.

If you care enough for the result,
you will most certainly attain it.

—WILLIAM JAMES

I began smoking when I was fifteen or sixteen. There was nothing more glamorous than Rita Hayworth slinking into a room with a long cigarette holder, or more romantic than Bette Davis accepting a lighted cigarette from Paul Henreid. I became a master in justifying why I needed a cigarette. They became a crutch, a shield, an extension of myself every minute of every day.

Fifty years later, I was still addicted. I had tried changing brands; hypnosis; acupuncture; stop smoking seminars; the patch; the pill; you name it. I could not stop. I wanted a magic wand. I was angry at myself, but never lost hope of finding a way to quit.

Then I came across a flyer for Nicotine Anonymous. A phone call changed my life. I began going to meetings and for over a year I slowly moved toward the day I could stop.

I will never forget that night; it was December 31, 2000 almost midnight, freezing cold, and there I was trying to smoke the last cigarette of the year while negotiating a glass of champagne with the other hand, mittens, scarf, hat and all. All of a sudden, it struck me that I was not enjoying the cigarette, the situation was beyond ridiculous. At long last, I was able to put them away. I am now approaching the third anniversary of freedom. Words cannot express how grateful I am to our Program and to the group that helped and supported my struggle to reach my goal.

Today, I am a truly happy person, enjoying to the fullest the experiences of life: its scents, flavors, everything.

MAY 18

There are risks and costs to a program of action.
But they are far less than the long range risks and
costs of comfortable inaction.
—JOHN F. KENNEDY

I may have used nicotine to feel more comfortable. I was not at ease
with myself or my world. Addiction is a dis-ease that seeks comfort
rather than courage.

Recovery asks me to take reasonable risks outside of my comfort
zone. I ask for the wisdom to know the difference between what to
accept and what to change.

Taking action may be uncomfortable. However, the competence
gained provides a comfort based on boldness rather than avoidance.
Though action may risk a pain or a defeat, the attitude of inaction only
maintains my need to anesthetize my anxiety and shame with nicotine.

My Program of recovery offers me a support system and Steps of
action. At my own pace, I came off the inactive list and engaged in the
action of living.

Today, I have comfort and peace because I
took risks to be clean and clear.

Every adult is in need of help, of warmth, of
protection, in many ways differing and yet in
many ways similar to the needs of a child.

—ERICH FROMM

Ninety percent of nicotine addicts started using tobacco as children. Some of us sought a sense of belonging with our peers. Smokers were an easily identifiable group. The burning ash offered a sense of warmth. The cloud of smoke felt protective. A cigarette provided something to hold onto.

"Smoking stunts your growth" is a phrase I heard as a kid. I discovered it is quite true when applied to my emotional and spiritual growth. It also hindered me from developing healthier coping skills.

As an adult I still need help, warmth, and protection. Our Fellowship offers me a caring place to fit and "re-form" myself. As I work my Program, I learn healthier behavior. Living without nicotine, my body breathes safely and stronger; my mind opens more clearly; my spirit rises more hopefully. With recovery, I grow beyond my childhood insecurities and tend to my real adult needs.

Today, with the guidance of the Twelve Steps and a Higher Power, I am learning how to take care of myself, "one day at a time."

Difficulties are meant to rouse, not discourage.
The human spirit is to grow strong by conflict.
—WILLIAM ELLERY CHANNING

Spirituality is a connection that transcends. Nicotine is a poison that pollutes. When I was "smogged" in smoke, my ability to have real contact with my Higher Power was diminished. When I used nicotine to escape, I removed myself. When I run away from what is, I end up with what is not.

Like the earth, we are embraced by air. We must continually inhale it to exist. This precious air is a constant universal connection to the life force.

When I depended on nicotine, I was denying faith an opportunity to reveal its full power. Faith does not come in a pack of cigarettes, or in dip or snuff. Faith needs to be exercised in order to be experienced.

Today, I choose to move toward the living
Spirit of my understanding, rather than
disappear into the deadening smoke.

Many things are lost for want of asking.

—ENGLISH PROVERB

During the last twenty years of my smoking I wanted to quit but did not. I believed there was not anything that could really help me. Smoking was my problem. I had put cigarettes into my mouth, so it was up to me to take them out. There were no gimmicks or tricks that could work for me.

I thought that I had to have more willpower. Since that never happened, it just reinforced the notion that I could not succeed. To even talk about setting a goal of quitting seemed like it would only invite ridicule when I failed.

Then I found this Fellowship. After attending meetings for seven months my way, I was struck with a deep sadness about my inability to stop smoking while other members could. It was then that I made my first serious and silent plea to a Power greater than myself, asking for help. I did not like the feeling at first, but it was my true beginning toward humility and finding freedom from nicotine.

Today, I will remember how much I've gained because I admitted I needed help from a Power greater than myself.

We cannot seek to attain health, wealth, learning
... in general. Action is always specific, concrete,
individualized, unique.

—JOHN DEWEY

The advantage of being involved in this Program of recovery is that it continually focuses my attention on defined courses of action that have helped so many other addicts. The actions involve my body, mind, and spirit. Action is essential to recovery for me as a nicotine addict.

Nicotine and tar are sticky and kept me stuck to my belief of inaction. Merely being busy with thoughts may simply disguise my fear of actually moving forward. Taking action gives me direct feedback. I realize firsthand what works and what does not.

Recovery guides me to ask for the courage to change the things I can. Practicing the principles of the Twelve Steps provides me with a specific, concrete, individualized, unique path to follow. These actions offer me freedom from nicotine and result in a spiritual awakening.

Today, I will take specific actions for my recovery, knowing there are certain rewards possible for me.

MAY 23

Keep away from people who try to belittle your
ambitions ... the really great [people] make you
feel that you, too, can become great.

—MARK TWAIN

Some of the most important things I get at meetings are the
"experience, strength and hope" of others. My previous bondage
now transforms into our new bond. We share a history with the
insanity of active behavior and, now, the enthusiasm of a new hope. This
common experience allows me to be inspired in a positive manner. I am
encouraged, not by shame or nagging, but by the example and
compassion of fellow members.

Other people in my life may care, but may not be able to fully
understand. Some may think that their harshness will force us to quit. I
come from an addictive family system with an equilibrium that
sometimes feels threatened by my attempts to change and improve.
Sometimes the ones I expect the most from, can only offer the least.
Recovery requires me to make wise choices about who is on the team
toward my dream.

*Today I will look to see how I can give and receive inspiration
within my Fellowship and surround myself with support.*

There is a place in us that can never be tarnished.

—PIR VILAYAT INAYAT KHAN

Meetings are where I "came to believe." I found that deep down in my heart, beyond the craving and shame of my addiction, is the hope to live my life without nicotine.

There are physical, emotional and spiritual consequences to this addiction. Just the constant repetitive behavior made it so difficult to even claim I had any hope. However, by heeding our slogan to "keep coming back," meetings became a place to nurture my hope. I admitted that I do want to prevent more of tobacco's damaging impact on my body and spirit. I do desire to live with the courage to engage with life rather than sneak around it. I do have a place within me that is untarnished, and it hopes.

The more clean time I experience, the more my hope has room to breathe. When I stopped putting nicotine and tar in, my "un-tar-nished" place began to show its face. I could actually see a radiance return to my skin. Yes, it is true, life shines.

Today, I choose not to use nicotine and to honor
the light of hope that shines within me.

When you fall, don't look where you fell. Look
where you slipped.

—AFRICAN PROVERB

When I struggle, when I am feeling like a failure, I try not to
stay in that feeling. I want to know what led me to the
struggle or the feeling of failure. It is actually kind of
interesting to play detective, to look for the clues and to put the case
together. By taking the problem apart I can understand how it came
together. This understanding may help me avoid a similar struggle or
failure happening again.

Today, I will use difficulty as an opportunity
for discovery and growth.

> He that will believe only what he can fully
> comprehend must have a very long head or a very
> short creed.
>
> —C.C. COLTON

In this Program of recovery I hear that "miracles happen." As a newcomer, I liked the idea, but did not really believe it. As a nicotine addict, I was accustomed to the instant solution I could grip in my hand. Accepting a possibility I could not grasp used to be beyond my capability.

Now, the more time I spend clean, the clearer I see the world around me. With the wall of smoke gone, I can witness more of nature's beauty. I smell it, I taste it, I touch it. I can now celebrate the creation. I am no longer trying to hide from this marvel called life.

The first miracle I recognized was that I had actually stopped using nicotine. This was just the beginning of my amazement. By coming to meetings I have come to believe in possibilities which no longer require an explanation to appreciate.

Today, miracles may not necessarily be something that I can grasp, but I am learning to embrace them.

It all depends on how we look at things, and not
on how they are in themselves.

—C.G. JUNG

Whether a day brings good news or bad, sunny skies or overcast, the ability to live more moments "happy, joyous, and free" will largely be determined by my attitude toward life's situations. My attitude becomes my personal experience each moment and determines what I will carry into the next moment.

The Serenity Prayer helps me ask for the courage I need to change. In recovery I pay more attention to the attitude I choose because that is what I can change about an experience.

Step Four helps me look at how I reacted to the things in the past. Many of my habitual patterns no longer serve me very well, if at all. Practicing Step Ten, I evaluate how my present attitudes and actions affect my life.

I ask for the serenity to accept "life on life's terms." I acknowledge that what's important is how I choose to respond to life. I focus on adjusting myself, not on altering reality with nicotine.

Today, I will choose the tones that color my world.

If you are patient in one moment of anger, you
will escape a hundred days of sorrow.
—CHINESE PROVERB

To live my life without the deadening effects of nicotine requires me to improve my relationship skills. Appropriately handling the inevitable moments of anger, with others or myself, is often a new challenge. I want to deal with feelings, not brandish them like a sword. Attacks on others can lead to guilt and negative attitudes about myself, which might brew an excuse to pick up nicotine.

As I become more conscious of my behavior, I learn there are critical moments of choice. I seek the wisdom to know when to let go and when to draw the line.

Sometimes denial or arrogance let me ignore the consequences of my addictive actions. Step Eight's list of amends now helps me acknowledge the reality of consequences. I am learning the difference between a childish reaction and a mature response. I am taking responsibility for my life and utilizing the power of choice.

Today, I will take the time to consider my principles and choose my response to life's situations.

Awakening begins when a man realizes that he is
going nowhere and does not know where to go.
—GEORGE GURDJIEFF

Despair and confusion are not barren. Within them can be the seeds of change. If it were not for reaching the end of my rope, I might never have let go. Pain is not necessarily negative unless I resist accepting its message. Maybe I had to get completely lost before I could surrender enough to admit I needed help, to pull over and ask for directions.

Step Twelve speaks of having a spiritual awakening as a result of these Steps. The point that can initiate change is often when a sense of despair and confusion overwhelms my status quo. I may only change when it is more uncomfortable to remain the same than it is to change.

Before recovery, I usually tried to solve problems by using more nicotine. Now, I can make healthier choices. With help from a Power greater than myself, I step forward into the process and find a new path.

Today, if my way is leading nowhere, I can pray for the
courage to open the door marked "change."

Some go through a forest and see no firewood.

—ENGLISH PROVERB

There may have been inspiration all around me, but I was so shrouded in smoke I could not see it. I was not able to be in real meaningful contact with other people, the beauty in nature, or a Higher Power. I was limited, stunted, turned inward in a way that kept me from noticing all that life offers.

Working my Program can help me to access the resources that are available. The "experience, strength and hope" of our Fellowship provide understanding and support. With this firewood I get the warmth and light I need.

As I recover, I see there is even value in my addiction. Cravings can urge me to use the tools of this Program. Cravings can be a signal that I need to take care of myself in some manner. I find that even the debris of addiction can be utilized to shed some light on where I need to look.

Today, I will open my eyes with a new clarity and realize the value of what is all around me.

MAY 31

Mastery consists of never giving in to self-pity.
—PIR VILAYAT INAYAT KHAN

Sometimes the closest I came to experiencing intimacy with myself was self-pity. Self-pity welcomes the deadness of smoking. Self-pity provides a list of justifications for why I continually put poisons into my body.

In recovery I can listen to the conversations in my mind in a new way. If I include the voice of my Higher Power there can be a new sanity and hope. If all I hear is my own voice there is a good chance I will indulge in familiar patterns of self-pity and put nicotine in my body.

When working Step Eight, I consider all those affected by this attitude. Step Ten helps me to remain vigilant about playing the victim. Self-pity is a poor substitute for care and it promotes inaction.

Self-pity, like nicotine, may have soothed me temporarily, but it can never truly satisfy me.

Today, I choose not to be a victim of my own design, and so I pray for my self-pity to be lifted, so that I may practice self-love.

Three things cannot long be hidden:
the sun, the moon, and the truth.
—CONFUCIOUS

One of the strengths of this recovery Program is that it understands no one really appreciates being told what to do. We seek and offer understanding and support. At meetings we are free to take what we want, and leave the rest.

With the help of a sponsor and a Higher Power, we each make choices and risk mistakes for ourselves. We each take responsibility for our lives. We watch, we listen, and notice healthy examples. Members are guided to identify with one another rather than to compare or judge. We walk our own path, resisting the temptation to tell other members how they should step.

My recovery is a personal process that is best shared, not sold.

Today, I will keep the focus on myself,
and let others choose their own path.

Ask not what your country can do for you, but
what you can do for your country.

—JOHN F. KENNEDY

S ervice within Nicotine Anonymous is a tool of recovery. Volunteers
are no longer victims. This Fellowship survives because people are
willing to offer service. Our recovery survives because we have a
Fellowship to serve. We are trying to nourish ourselves back from a
deadening disease. What better activity than to tend to the garden that
feeds us.

Service also makes amends toward the world in general. Addiction
has sickened and burdened societies. Each recovering person adds to the
healing. When anyone rises to recovery, all are elevated.

Working the Twelfth Step, we "carry the message" of Nicotine
Anonymous to nicotine users. When our focus is on expanding our
Fellowship, we are less likely to focus on feeling deprived. We stay more
in touch with what we gain rather than on anything lost. To serve the
Fellowship that unifies us is to connect to a source of strength. To shrink
to the merely me is to withdraw into isolation.

Today, I will find a way to serve others.

The part can never be well
unless the whole is well.

—PLATO

Nicotine was my first drug addiction, but it was the last to go. I thought putting down my other drugs was hard, but nicotine is the toughest. I had learned to work the Steps in another Program, but I had to make an enormous leap of faith to become willing to live without nicotine.

I needed a Fellowship that focuses specifically on nicotine. Even scientific studies have proven that nicotine is one of the most powerfully addictive substances.

Exchanging nicotine for the care of a Higher Power did not come easily for me. Once I truly accepted, that I alone cannot control my use of nicotine, I could begin asking for help. As I became willing to receive my Higher Power's care, the fear diminished that kept me clenched with resistance. Then, living without nicotine became possible. Surrendering my diseased body and mind to spiritual care is the solution.

Today, I watch for signs that I am resisting surrendering my life and my will. If I cannot immediately release my control, I will pray for willingness.

I have not failed. I've just found ten
thousand ways that won't work.

—THOMAS ALVA EDISON

Using nicotine kept me stuck in a discouraging cycle. It seemed that no matter what I thought or did, I could not get off the "despair-go-round."

However, in meetings I witnessed others' actions of hope, and I wanted to set a quit date. I still had to wrestle with doubt and delay. Doubt and delay were colluding cousins in my addictive system.

Preparing for and setting a quit date was like casting out a rescue line. It was an attempt to hook something solid so I could pull myself from the quicksand. When the day came that I did not make it, I looked for lessons, coiled up my line, set another date, and cast again.

There are no failures, just attempts. Attempts were valuable practice. The addict voice in my head chattered with discouragement. It did not want me to break free. I found I could acknowledge that voice, but not obey it. When I finally got free, I found that none of the noise mattered.

Today, if I need to, I can be like the spider,
and spin another web to catch my dream.

I prayed to have this obsession with smoking
lifted, then added, "God, could you please make it
easy for this weak addict."

—NICOTINE ANONYMOUS MEMBER

When I heard this plea, I was taken by surprise. Could someone make such a request? I witnessed week by week how it worked for her. This request helped her quit after thirty-five years of chain smoking. Her example made me look at the expectation I had erected and the limits I had imposed.

Wasn't withdrawal supposed to be unbearable? Could there be power in the act of asking? After I witnessed months of her process and progress, how could I deny it?

Working a Step Four on this attitude, I saw my investment. If quitting was different from what I had believed, than maybe I could have quit years ago. I also discovered that my shame believed that quitting should not be easy.

I see now that it had been more important to maintain my being right than to be free. "Working the Steps" shows me there can be new possibilities when I am willing to set aside my pride and my shame.

*Today, I accept that my struggles can be eased if I
am willing to let go of my old investments.*

Nodding the head does not row the boat.
—IRISH PROVERB

R ecovery takes more than gestures and half-hearted attempts to get me across troubled waters. If I have given only lip service in my past efforts, the words were merely hollow places to hide excuses.

As a nicotine addict, I used the deception of smoke and mirrors. Smoking may have looked like I was busy, but it was just a lot of hot air.

Maintaining recovery requires more than just agreement that I should do this, or I ought to do that. Recovery requires my sincere participation. Sincerity brings a power with it. If I want to change the scene I have to pull on the oars and do the work.

Today, I am grateful that this recovery Program
has given me tasks to do, tasks with a purpose.

If the person you are talking to doesn't appear to
be listening, be patient. It may simply be that he
has a small piece of fluff in his ear.
—"WINNIE THE POOH," BY A. A. MILNE

L ike many other newcomers I did not jump at the chance to sit at a
meeting with strangers for an hour without using tobacco. I was
uncomfortable admitting I had failed to quit on my own. It took a
while to see how members offer understanding, not criticism.

I did have a trusting relationship with groups or a Power greater
than myself. After all, I had used nicotine to gain more control over my
life, not to surrender it. The reality that I might actually be separated
from my best buddy was definitely scary. Any type of discomfort had
always been an excuse to use.

However, because I was willing to show up for our recovery, I found
hope. The more I witnessed this hope around me, the more I wanted to
exchange it for the despair I had known all too well. In Step Two, I came
to believe. Liking meetings was a process as well. In accepting my initial
discomfort, I found that I actually came to enjoy meetings.

*Today, I accept that crossing a bridge of discomfort
can bring me to a new place of joy.*

Love of certainty is a demand for
guarantees in advance of action.

—JOHN DEWEY

I had used nicotine in an attempt to control emotional responses to the situations I encountered. The anxiety of some impending uncertainty was just too overwhelming. My reflex was to medicate my feelings with nicotine rather than to meditate with faith. I sought security through nicotine's instant guarantee.

An obstacle that I imposed on even the idea of quitting was that I wanted to be certain that I would not fail. Because my constant smoking was so visible to others, any attempt to stop would be obvious to my friends and family. Therefore, a failure to quit would be known to all. I felt enough shame about my inability to stop, and I did not want more when I failed. Resigned, I also took odd comfort in that certainty of failure.

I craved the certainty along with the nicotine. The result was that I took no action, and thus created no hope. I had not yet asked for the serenity and courage that would change my life.

Today, I am coming to believe that I cannot control every outcome with certainty. I can, with faith, take action, create hope, and find peace that I sought for years.

There is no such thing as a long piece of work,
except one that you dare not start.
—CHARLES BAUDELAIRE

Once, the reality of reaching freedom from nicotine seemed too far to attain, and too tough to maintain. My words to whine with were, "What's the use, it's just too hard." I would also excuse my inaction with, "Not now, I have to wait until...." Procrastination can make waiting last forever.

Practicing our Program's principles, I find I can deal with challenges better when I do not indulge in how large or long a task may be. Instead, my goal is to simply move forward, even if it is just a little bit, toward the next moment. I focus on the present and just "do the next right thing."

Each time I make some progress at anything in front of me, I strengthen my courage for future efforts. Like the principle of inertia, movement tends to keep going in the direction it is headed.

Today, I may not be able to stride the whole distance,
but I can take a step, seeking "progress not perfection."

No music in the world is more beautiful than the ringing of
church bells heard from a distance over an open country.
—LLEWELYN POWYS

I really welcomed the honesty heard during meetings. I could connect
and find hope in both the struggle of others and their strengths.
These were not voices that condemned me. They neither pushed nor
prodded me. Though I had never heard this music before, I was drawn to
the sweet surrender of its calling.

I had to travel quite a distance to attend meetings, but the
"experience, strength and hope" offered by fellow members was worth
the effort. The meetings are out there or they can be started. The need is
calling all over the land.

Whether by the manner of my interactions or by posting meeting
flyers, Step Twelve asks me to "carry the message," to help let all those
who seek freedom from nicotine know there is help.

*Today, I want to be a part of the music that brings
hope to the ears of others seeking recovery.*

If you are bitter at heart, sugar in
the mouth will not help you.
—YIDDISH PROVERB

Nicotine may have stuffed my anger, but this created a breeding ground for bitterness and resentment. These attitudes are threats to my recovery.

Bitterness can have a deep root. Steps Four through Nine are there to find it, admit it, ask to have it lifted, and make an amends about it. Bitterness and resentment are not things I can clean up with a once-over swipe. I usually need to get down on my knees.

I improve my chances of keeping clean of tobacco's toxins when I keep myself clean of emotional poisons. The Steps are guidelines for clean living. To more fully enjoy the benefits of recovery, I need to work Step Six to become entirely ready for any bitterness to be lifted. I do this so I can move on with my life with a light heart. I want to make room for the love I need to heal.

*Today, I will take Steps to be clean so that I might
taste that true sweetness of life and love.*

Aahhh, to the day.

—NICOTINE ANONYMOUS MEMBER

After the initial days of withdrawal's pangs I began experiencing moments of wonderment's pleasure. When I start my day with recovering lungs and returning senses, I can say, "Aahhh, to the day." Without the deadening effects of all the toxic smoke I once sucked in, my body can rediscover the pleasure of aroma and flavor. As an adult I had never known them, especially the subtle ones. Recovering my senses was like a child's birthday, full of new toys to enjoy.

I recovered my sense of sanity. Withdrawal was confusing at first, but with time I found a new clarity. I had removed a shame from my life. I now feel more presentable and can greet each morning with, "Aahhh, to the day."

The more I experience the freedom from my addiction, the more I feel encouraged to celebrate. It had been a long time since I felt this good, this deeply.

Today, I have come to my senses, and I
celebrate all of life's pleasures.

JUNE 13

Talk doesn't cook rice.

—CHINESE PROVERB

Talking has both positive and negative aspects. It is beneficial when it is an honest expression of what I feel. It can be an opportunity to come out of those isolated places I used to hide in. This enhanced my ability to be more intimate with others and even with myself. I also keep my recovery by sharing it at meetings. Talking is one of my medicines.

However, talking alone does not necessarily get the job done. The mannerisms of my addiction provided me with a means to look busy, to seem involved, when I really was not. Sometimes, talking may be another smoke screen to hide behind. I had a pattern of fooling others and myself.

I have learned the value of vigilance. I take care to measure the integrity in my actions as well as the ingredients in my words.

Today, I will be watchful that I do not disguise myself in my words, and see that my deeds speak for me.

Boasting is not courage.

—AFRICAN PROVERB

Tobacco products can be used as a dramatic prop. While smoking, I could blow out a big puff to be demonstratively expressive. Spitting tobacco flakes also made quite a statement. In either case, it did not necessarily mean that I had either power or courage. Often I used my habit to disguise a lack of self-confidence.

I used to brag like daredevils. Heck, I was not afraid of diseases like cancer and emphysema. My false bravado had me hoping I could show off at ninety by saying, "see, I told you so."

Once my brain was free from nicotine, I began to realize I had risked a lot for very little. Recovery offers me more worthwhile accomplishments that provide real satisfaction.

Today, I am humbly impressed with my
courage to live my life without nicotine.

Our own physical body possesses a wisdom which
we who inhabit the body lack. We give it orders
which make no sense.

—HENRY MILLER

When I was using nicotine, my body was in conflict with my actions. In spite of denial, my organs knew they were being invaded by poison. They struggled constantly to clear out the crap I kept shoving in. My body's incredible ability to withstand this abuse allowed me to continue the damaging behavior, but it also held on with a hope.

When I stopped using nicotine, my mind and body realized I was being restored to sanity and begin to make repairs. Vitality returned. I added my body to my Step Eight list and made amends with proper exercise, good food, and sufficient rest.

Now, I can sense more of my body's wisdom. My body is no longer consumed with the insane battle of self-destruction. I have become clearer about when I am "hungry, angry, lonely, or tired." I experience a keener intuitive sense, when my inner ear is open.

Today, I will respect my body's knowledge.
When it speaks, I will listen.

A book is like a garden carried in the pocket.
—CHINESE PROVERB

R eading recovery literature is one of our Program's tools. I am nourished by the "experience, strength and hope" of its pages. A book is also a wonderful way for me as a recovering addict to spend quiet time. I needed to find ways of being at ease with myself when I was not involved in daily busyness. Carrying a book, rather than tobacco, is good for break periods.

Like a garden, reading can provide me with a diverse array of possibilities. Literature can expand my knowledge and humanity.

Now, free from the activities of my addiction, I have more time for myself. Reading can be a healthy way to spend some of the time I have saved.

Today, I can take the time to learn something
new at my own pace, one page at a time.

JUNE 17

When you reread a classic you do not see more in
the book than you did before; you see more in
you than was there before.

—CLIFTON FADIMAN

It is valuable to keep digging in my mine. Each day I recommit to continue the thorough search of my personal inventory. By separating the rocks from the gems, I become richer for the effort.

Recovery literature is one of my tools. Like a shovel, it helps me discover what is in my depths. I have layers, books have their pages.

On any given day, my mood influences the meaning I discover. Although the words do not change their point of view, I do.

Like many tobacco users I had been burying myself for years with layers of nicotine. I now work this Program daily, not only because of the challenges in front of me, but because of what is behind me. As a recovering addict, I am like archeologists. I am seeking out my artifacts. What were the reasons I picked up this addiction? What has been buried under the numbness? What strengths of character have I overlooked? As the silts of shame are lifted I am discovering that I have fascinating depths to explore.

*Today, I will review the Steps I have already
taken so that I may leave no stone unturned.*

One of the worst forms of mental suffering is boredom,
not knowing what to do with oneself and one's life.
—ERICH FROMM

Tricky triggers for me like some other nicotine addicts, are those pauses, those breaks between, when I feel bored. At the time, I may have felt them to be agonizingly long, even when they may have been mere seconds. My dis-ease with myself pushed me to fill the space. I did, with nicotine. My anxiety was relieved as I busied myself with my familiar tobacco rituals.

During pauses my internal dialogue becomes more audible. The reality of my addictive behavior is more apparent. I sometimes feared a moment of truth was at hand, so I would stick a stick of numb in my mouth to silence the message. I was, and sometimes still may be, uneasy with intimacy, with others and myself.

There are also aspects of this addiction that create boredom. Tobacco use is sticky, smoggy, suffocating, numbing, isolating, limiting, just to name a few. This has a constant stifling influence. Boredom breeds when I do not move. Boredom leads to more boredom. How boring.

Today, in my own way, I can meditate instead of medicate to bring peace to my pauses and inspiration to my activities.

Any change, even a change for the better, is always
accompanied by drawbacks and discomforts.

—ARNOLD BENNETT

This is an honest Program. When I have a craving for nicotine and choose not to use, I will have moments of discomfort. These physical and emotional sensations can be difficult to manage. However, I find that the experience is not as bad as I had expected.

Coming to terms with the discomfort has a lot to do with accepting the craving. I am not served in the long run if I try to wrestle with or deny the craving. Nicotine use made my body crave more nicotine, and my mind became obsessed with it. These are the facts.

When I accepted my short term discomfort in exchange for the long term benefits, I found myself at the threshold of change. When I truly accept reality, I can stop struggling and resisting change. Surrender opens me to connect to a real energy. With this energy I can choose not to use.

*Today, I accept that even change for the better has uncomfortable
moments, and these will pass whether I use nicotine or not.*

It is the province of knowledge to speak, and it is
the privilege of wisdom to listen.

—OLIVER WENDELL HOLMES

When I was a newcomer, I had to assess whether this Program could be helpful to me. Some of the phrases seemed strange. I was put off by the frequent mention of God and Higher Power. Let's be real. Lots of people just stop using nicotine cold turkey. What has religion got to do with quitting? I was surprised that you did not expect to be cured in two or three meetings. Some of you had been coming to meetings for years.

You made we welcome. Beyond that, you encouraged me to express my thoughts. You did not judge anything I said. Some of you meet separately with me to focus completely on my questions and issues. I remember my first meeting, and how I felt overwhelmed by attention. You gave me a few pieces of literature which I really appreciated. You recommended that I attend six meetings before deciding whether Nicotine Anonymous was right for me. I was willing to try six meetings, though I did not plan to hang around for years.

You assured me Nicotine Anonymous was not a religious Program. You told me that you believed that the nicotine addiction had affected you emotionally, physically, and spiritually. I found that my recovery did actually depend on healing and growing in all three dimensions. You assured me I could interpret spiritual growth and a Higher Power in a way that was personally acceptable. What a relief to discover that I did not have to do it all on my own. You told me I could rely on the group to be my Higher Power.

*Today, I can turn to the God of my understanding, or
use the experience of the group to help me recover.*

Doubt yourself and you doubt everything you see.
Judge yourself and you see judges everywhere. But if
you listen to the sound of your own voice, you can rise
above doubt and judgment. And you can see forever.

—NANCY KERRIGAN

I used to believe using tobacco looked glamorous and appealing. I believed that users were young, healthy men and women living life to its fullest. I believed tobacco would make me seductive. I saw tobacco as a fashion accessory. Tobacco represented rebellion, sobriety, sophistication and maturity. I had allowed tobacco to define who I was.

What I was really doing was ingesting poison. That was the reality of my addiction. Irrespective of what symbols I created for myself, positive or negative, using tobacco was simply a nasty addiction, nothing more.

Nicotine Anonymous helped me see through those lies to the truth about my addiction. Today, I wonder how I could have believed those images.

*Today I will stretch my limits, forget about
the past and concentrate on today.*

One of the griefs of my life is to see other persons
getting things done, really done, and I accomplish
so little. I don't see how they do it.

—CLARA BARTON

Rarely do I have the sense that anything I accomplish makes a real
difference in the world. Why do I dismiss my accomplishments,
comparing myself unfavorably to others? Trapped in the despair
of my nicotine addiction, I did not dare look deeply at who I am. I felt
insignificant.

This morning as I was meditating, I focused on my painting of
dandelions. I realized it is ordinary for the roots to reach deeply into the
soil, for the leaves to accept sunlight, for the flower to produce a seed
ball, for the sun to produce light, for the dirt to receive moisture and
nutrients, for the wind to blow. All these ordinary events produce and
reproduce hardy plants. To achieve extraordinary plants, all that is
required is a change in one of those elements.

Sunlight cannot substitute for rain, nor can rain compensate for lack
of sunlight. Success does not mean I have to force myself to accomplish
tasks for which I lack talents or skills. I only have to focus and do my
best at any given moment, regardless of what my best is on any given
day.

As I learn to appreciate myself, I can accept others just as they are. I
am not meant to be a dandelion; a dandelion is not meant to be a
mountain; everyone and everything is meant to be exactly as God
created.

*Today, I remember that who and what I am is exactly in
accordance with God's plan for my life.*

Do not dwell in the past, do not dream of the future,
concentrate the mind on the present moment.
—BUDDHA

I lived my life looking forward to my next nicotine hit: after dinner, after work, after a doctor's appointment, etc. Therefore the idea of looking ahead at possibly decades of nothing to look forward to was really depressing. That's why the slogans, "just for today" and "one day at a time" really worked for me. I soon found other small but healthy pleasures to look forward to.

Today, I will remember that I cannot get through quitting nicotine by using nicotine.

Success is simple. Do what's right,
the right way, at the right time.
—ARNOLD H. GLASOW

I am glad and grateful I am not using nicotine because:
I am happier
I am more free
I do not have to pay $15 a day
I do not have to pay $160 for sinusitis prescriptions
I am not owned by nicotine
I can go to non-smoking areas without apprehension about when I
    will have that next cigarette
I look forward to not using nicotine
I can live "one day at a time" with God's grace.

*Today, I will focus on all the reasons
I am grateful.*

Cast your cares on the Lord and he will sustain
you; he will never let the righteous fall.
—THE BIBLE

D o I hold God or nicotine as my companion? When I am using
nicotine, I have no room in my life for a Higher Power.
Nicotine completely preoccupies me. I major in it. The most
important thing in my day is nicotine. Sometimes it is my only activity. I
just sit or pace the floor feeding my addiction.

I want to be close to God. I want to leave room in my life for
him/her. It is very dysfunctional having nicotine be my Higher Power
rather than the real deal.

The Twelve Steps teach me to focus on improving myself and
working on becoming closer to God. I want God to be my Higher
Power, not a substance such as nicotine. I give over my addiction to
him/her, therefore I can maintain my abstinence. My Higher Power can
do for me what I cannot do for myself.

Today, I choose God as my companion.

It is one of the most beautiful compensations of
this life that no man can sincerely try to help
another without helping himself
—RALPH WALDO EMERSON

As I lost my best friend, nicotine, I felt isolated. The feeling of loneliness was there every time I ran out of my nicotine source. In reality, I have never been alone.

Today I am not alone. I have made the decision to let go of all the negative feelings I have that nicotine ever helped. Nicotine only gave me a false security blanket of comfort.

By helping myself, I am clearing a path in my forest of negative feelings to enable me to help others. It is helping others that enables me to do the work of Step Twelve and to participate in the joy of living. I see this joy in every Nicotine Anonymous member who shares themselves with others. I am working Step Twelve by letting go of myself.

Today, I am grateful for the years Nicotine Anonymous has added to my life and for the life in my years.

JUNE 27

Action is the foundational key to all success.
—PABLO PICASSO

I have had many dreams that I was still using nicotine, even after I stopped. Each dream had a common theme, the realization that I was still using, and the attempt to rationalize that I had not lost my time free from nicotine.

I would lie to myself, but then surrender to the idea that I had to restart my time. More importantly, I had to restart my day. In the dreams I know that acceptance is the only solution. When I awoke I was always relieved to find I have not gone back to my addiction. Only through acceptance and positive action has my situation changed. As I keep current, I do not crave nicotine, neither awake nor asleep.

Today, I will focus only on today.
Tomorrow does not count.

The ladder of success is best climbed by
stepping on the rungs of opportunity.
—AYN RAND

With nicotine no longer masking my feelings, I need to pay
attention to my emotional life and learn how to act effectively
on my feelings. Emotional upheavals could provide an excuse
to use nicotine again if I am not careful how I choose to respond.

To avoid relapse, it is important to attend meetings regularly, so I am
reminded of how life used to be when I was using nicotine. I also need to
talk about how my life is now, to be reminded of why I chose not to use
nicotine today.

When I contrast how my life used to be with how it is now, it helps
me activate gratitude to my Higher Power for lifting the terrible burden
of nicotine addiction. My Higher Power has done for me what I was
unable to do for myself. The freedom I experience being nicotine-free is
beyond words.

---

*Today, I compare my life before and after freedom from nicotine,
and I am grateful for the help of my Higher Power.*

Good judgment comes from experience, and often
experience comes from bad judgment.
—RITA MAE BROWN

E ach time I fed my nicotine addiction it did not really bring me pleasure, because pleasure to an addict is merely relief from discomfort. Every day I remember that not using nicotine is uncomfortable only temporarily and for a short period of time. Using nicotine is uncomfortable eternally.

I had to get honest. I wanted to continue using nicotine. That is the truth. However, I had the choice to use or not. I always had the choice to continue what I had been doing. I can choose to tread the waters of nicotine addiction, or just for this moment, I can choose the nicotine-free path. That is a path that may be unknown, but it is my path to freedom. When I was at the crossroads, I chose the path to freedom.

Making that choice was not about willpower, it was about choice. Choice is an action that occurs now, in this moment. Am I going to make the choice to use nicotine or to embrace freedom?

*Today, I remember that withdrawal is the feeling I
experience as my body and mind are healing.*

To conquer fear is the beginning of wisdom.
—BERTRAND RUSSELL

The order of the day is sitting, resting, waiting for the right opportunity to miss out on pain. The bonds of nicotine addiction are too great to break without a God who will lead and remove the pain of my past mistakes and desires. God removed the pain and hopelessness.

The old pioneers of all Twelve Step Programs provide understanding and compassion. They are forces in the universe that come together and deliver me from pain.

Today, I remember that God
is always ready when I am.

Success is dependent on effort.

—SOPHOCLES

Being a member of other Twelve Step Fellowships enhanced my chances in Nicotine Anonymous. I had eighteen years in Alcoholics Anonymous when I finally decided to try Nicotine Anonymous.

We use the same Higher Power. We use the same Steps even though it is a different addiction. I can use both Nicotine Anonymous and Alcoholics Anonymous meetings to keep me free of my addictions. I just finished thirty months free from nicotine.

Today, I will continue
working my Program.

JULY 2

Faith is putting all your eggs in God's basket, then
counting your blessings before they hatch.
—RAMONA C. CARROLL

When I look at it, I make many decisions every day. Habits help me decide certain things quickly, without much thought. I brush my teeth, a good habit. Or I use nicotine, a bad habit. Usually I do not think about these little decisions. I allow habits to rule.

When the issue is big, such as moving from where I live, I give the decision more thought. I try to figure it from every angle. Sometimes I make snap decisions, reacting to a comment or acting on a whim. I can make impulsive decisions because it causes anxiety to really examine the factors in a big decision.

As I take Step Three, I may make the decision again and again. Maybe one time I impulsively turn my will and life over during a time of crisis. Another time I may not see the result I want right away, so I take back the controls and stir things up.

*Today, I turn my life and my will over to my
Higher Power. Before I take it back, I will
stop and reaffirm Step Three.*

In faith there is enough light for those
who want to believe and enough
shadows to blind those who don't.

—BLAISE PASCAL

L ike many smokers, I had a hard time smoking my first cigarette. I got dizzy. The taste was strange. I choked and coughed the first time I inhaled, but I persisted.

The Steps are that way too. With experience, I learn more. I have a deeper understanding of how to apply the Steps in my life. Sometimes I go back to Step One, but then forget and take back the thinking that can control my addiction.

Step Two gains meaning for me over time too. As they say in another Twelve Step Program, "first I came, then I came to, finally I came to believe."

This is not a religion. I am discovering that a Power stronger than nicotine is active in my everyday life. This Power has the strength to break the nicotine obsession, if I allow it.

The addiction to and obsession with nicotine is a deadly form of insanity. Those are such harsh words for such a little vice. Really? Is it wrong to call a killer a deadly form of insanity?

*Today, I gladly allow a Power greater than myself
to break my obsession with nicotine.*

Freedom has many facets, but mostly it releases us
from much that has been troubling and defeating
us. We pray for this release into freedom.
—ONE DAY AT A TIME IN AL-ANON

When I was smoking, I thought that I was in control, but really it was the cigarette, really the nicotine in the cigarette, that was controlling me. Nicotine determined with whom I would travel, who would travel with me, even whether I would travel at all. Nicotine determined with whom I had relationships, and who would have them with me. It was these two themes around which my Higher Power led me back to Nicotine Anonymous. I was planning a trip to the south of France. The trip would involve not smoking for nine hours on the plane, and later traveling with non-smoking relatives. What complete and utter misery.

I was desperate and no longer wanted to suffer. In the rooms of Nicotine Anonymous, I found unconditional love, open arms, and the freedom to discover myself without the smothering blanket of nicotine. The people in the rooms held me as I learned to accept my powerlessness and not act on my cravings. I grabbed onto service as if it were a life preserver. I took lots of tools with me on my trip and did not smoke. I was able to experience many joyful moments as a result.

At the time of this writing, I am celebrating my fifth anniversary of freedom from nicotine, "one day at a time." It is a miracle beyond my wildest dreams, and I could not have done it alone. I owe this day to Nicotine Anonymous.

*Today, I will leave behind yesterday, not fear
tomorrow, and live in the freedom of today.*

No one can possibly be satisfied and no one can be
happy who feels that in some paramount affairs he
failed to take up the challenge of life.
—ARNOLD BENNETT

The Twelve Steps are the powerful backbone of my recovery. As I study the Steps, I gain insights that give me new freedoms and new guidance about living a full and rich life. I had been restricted by nicotine. I had lost some flexibility. But now I have a new gift, a grace, a set of exercises to strengthen and develop my character, free of my addiction.

Like an infant, I started with Step One. I recognize that the drug nicotine had me in its grip. All of my attempts to quit had failed. I could not manage the cravings. I was powerless, my health was damaged, I smelled, but I would go out in any circumstances to get nicotine if somehow I had run out. My life was truly unmanageable.

*Today, I remember that all living things continue
to change and grow until death.*

Wisdom denotes the pursuing of
the best ends by the best means.
—FRANCIS HUTCHESON

Trees grow by a ring that starts in the core and spreads out as the core creates again. We can examine the rings in any tree stump to find the story of that tree. Scientists can tell dry spells and good weather during the life of the tree by examining the thickness or thinness the rings.

When I take a moral inventory of myself in Step Four, I examine myself at one level, at least initially. As a new member of Nicotine Anonymous, I had the impact nicotine had on my health. It was most valuable to accept my inventory based on where I was at that time. As I progress in recovery I have gained greater insights. I am finding how my nicotine obsession kept me from being fully present with other people and avoiding uncomfortable feelings.

As I study the rings of my character again, I find that I was spiritually stunted in some surprising ways. I had been self-righteous, and I justified my action for years, but now I am seeing the truth. The Steps take on greater meaning as I grow in wisdom. I am becoming more able to apply the Steps to my life at levels closer to my core.

*Today, I continue to take my inventory, and I am
grateful for the wisdom that process brings me.*

> Y'know, chewing tobacco is an addiction,
> too. Just "don't quit quitting."
> —ALCOHOLICS ANONYMOUS MEMBER

Quitting is easy. I must have quit a hundred times. It's the staying quit I have difficulty with. My tobacco of choice is snuff/dip. After many failed attempts at staying quit; I felt resigned to continue dipping the rest of my life.

One day while talking with my friend about his struggle with alcohol and drugs, he pointed out that chewing tobacco was also an addiction. I found it difficult to accept myself as an addict. "I'm not an addict," I told him (and myself). He asked how many times I had tried to quit and how it has worked for me so far.

In the ensuing weeks, he was able to convince me to attend an Alcoholics Anonymous meeting with him and go back to a smoking cessation class, which led me to Nicotine Anonymous. In Nicotine Anonymous, I have come to learn and understand what addiction is and accept who I am, the good and the bad. I am an addict and I am not alone. I have found strength through others who share the same feelings, behaviors and struggles as myself.

I quit chewing tobacco almost four years ago, but staying quit is a life-long commitment.

Today, I choose to live my life, through the
good and the bad, without tobacco.

A friend is the only person you will let into the
house when you are turning out drawers.

—PAM BROWN

I hear people come into our meetings for the first time say something
like, "I had to quit. I had a heart attack." Mentally I always laugh. I
want to respond, "No you didn't." One time I quit was weeks before
part of my left lung was removed. After that I did not think I would start
again.

Three months later I had a really bad day at the office. I had changed
jobs in the interim and no one knew I was an addict. I walked into the
lunch room where two employees were smoking and that triggered my
tape. I started arguing against bumming a cigarette but my final argument
was, "if you drop dead on the spot, do you really want a cigarette?" My
answer was, "yes, if I have to feel like this, life isn't worth living."

I bummed one, and immediately went downstairs and bought a
carton.

For years I kept trying to quit. I would for a time but the day would
come when things were bad enough, or I had been good enough to
deserve one.

It took fourteen years to find Nicotine Anonymous. You helped me
see that I am doomed as soon as I begin the argument. You talked about
dealing with feelings rather than stuffing them. You were honest, and
allowed me to be honest. You loved me. Eventually I started discovering
who I am, instead of being who I thought others wanted me to be.

Today, when I see someone using nicotine,
I thank God I am free.

We cannot become what we need to be by
remaining what we are.

—MAX DEPREE

E arly in my recovery, I would listen to the Promises, and I was
very skeptical about, "we now realize we have been participating
in a grand hoax. We haven't given up anything at all." Now it is
my favorite promise.

Since I quit, I continue to realize dreams that had seemed impossible.
I can now: establish and enforce boundaries; sing; volunteer; have healthy
relationships; enjoy life; release old fears; be comfortable speaking
publicly; offer a warm welcome to strangers; express my opinion; let
others disagree; have a church community that I relish.

I can: be who I had always wished to be; go years without seeing a
doctor except for checkups; use nicotine savings on luxuries; not be
embarrassed by the odor of cigarettes; work on projects that take more
than a few minutes; exercise; shop for hours; enjoy movies and the
theater; enjoy traveling; go rafting, or canoeing; sit still; choose
employment based on my needs and desires since I no longer have to
plan on retiring by age fifty-five to have time to enjoy life before I die. I
started painting and discovered talent; I no longer cough; I am no longer
painfully shy.

I have more gains than there is room here to record. It is absolutely
true, I have not given up anything at all, except for shame, guilt, disease,
discomfort and a premature death.

Today, I am free to be me.

One today is worth two tomorrows.
—BENJAMIN FRANKLIN

The rewards of a nicotine-free life are manifest in all my senses. The color and clarity of my vision is astonishing. The reds, yellows and golds of the autumn trees are brighter to me today, and each nicotine-free day is another gift from the Power.

My contribution is to collect each day as it is given to me. Each day is a collection, like the stones of a great pyramid reaching for the light of the sky.

Today, I will take time to relish each minute.

If we could sell our experiences for what they cost
us, we'd all be millionaires.
—ABIGAIL VAN BUREN

I was in the sixth grade when I had my first cigarette. I coughed some, but immediately wanted another. My sister would not give me one because it might make me sick. From that point, I never got enough.

I used to take eight to ten-hour bus trips six times a year from the eighth grade through high school. Those were the times I could smoke freely. I would get a pack at my earliest opportunity, and would normally finish it during the trip. I did not want to look inexperienced, so I would watch other smokers to see when they lit up. Even then it seemed as though I had to wait forever between cigarettes.

By the end of my struggle with nicotine, I did not want anything to separate me from my cigarettes. I would have five cigarettes before getting dressed and another five during the three-mile drive to my office. I could no longer smoke at my desk so I would find excuses to get out of the office, sneak downstairs mid-morning and mid-afternoon. At home, I would sit chain smoking, trying to stop long enough to fix dinner, but keep bargaining for just one more. I would start craving my next one before I was half finished with the current one. I would frequently wake up in the middle of the night to have a few.

After years of struggling on my own, I found Nicotine Anonymous. You gave me hope.

*Today, I am free of the compulsion to feed
my addiction. I revel in my freedom.*

Experience is not what happens to you; it is what
you do with what happens to you.

—ALDOUS HUXLEY

L ast week a year-long romance ended. Nicotine will not help.
Yesterday I learned that my job will end this Friday. Nicotine will
not help. I hurt very badly, but nicotine will not help.

Today I will use every tool of the Program that I know. I will live
through just this one day, maybe taking it one hour at a time, or a minute
at a time. I will attend a meeting tonight. I will practice "letting go and
letting God." I may find myself taking my troubles back from the
Higher Power, because I have a hard time letting go of them. When I
catch myself, I will let go again.

I will take steps to find my right work where I can be productive,
express my talents, and earn a just income. I will trust that the world has
such a place where I am needed. My job is to find that right place.

---

*Today, I will consciously release the outcome and
concentrate only on doing the next right thing.*

Life must be understood backwards.
But it must be lived forward.

—SOREN KIERKEGAARD

I look for guideposts to tell me how I am doing and what to expect. When I found Nicotine Anonymous I wanted to know answers to the following questions:

How long will the physical withdrawal symptoms last?
What will they be like?
When will the cravings be bearable?
When will I stop feeling angry and out of control?
How long will I have to come to meetings?

I listened to others share their experiences. Sometimes it was confusing. Each speaker had such different things to say. After several meetings, I started to form some general ideas of what the Program is about. It is helping me live better in my own individual way. I have unique views to share with other addicts.

I am turned off occasionally. Members suggested that I visit different groups, and that I attend at least six meetings before judging whether the Program could help me. Members encouraged me to "take what I like and leave the rest."

Now I remember that joining a new group is uncomfortable for most people. I welcome newcomers, and let them know how Nicotine Anonymous has helped me. I tell them I am glad they came, and I encourage them to "keep coming back."

Today, I let go of trying to find answers for anyone but me. I am open to others' experience, and I am free to choose my own path.

The wise man must remember that while he is a
descendant of the past, he is a parent of the future.

—HERBERT SPENCER

I have seen many people come and go in the rooms of Nicotine
Anonymous and often wonder where people go, or how, or if they
stay nicotine-free.

For me, getting free of nicotine was the First Step, but in order to
live a life that is truly free, I have to work the rest of the Steps.

I came to Nicotine Anonymous thinking I knew the Steps having
come from a couple of other Twelve Step Programs. What I have learned
is that I had to surrender, become teachable, and work the Steps as a
newcomer who did not know anything about this new recovery.

The freedom I have received through "working the Steps" in
Nicotine Anonymous is unlike anything I have ever experienced. Not
only am I no longer a slave to nicotine, but I am mentally, emotionally,
and spiritually free.

Today, I know when I work the Steps
I find the path to freedom.

A man is about as happy
as he makes up his mind to be.
—ABRAHAM LINCOLN

H ere it is a brand new day, and I am grim and glum. What a waste of possibilities if I do not get past this attitude. Well a new day can start again at any time, so I am going to start again now. There will be funny things to laugh about today, if I let myself see them. I have work to do, certainly, and I have responsibilities to meet. That is no reason to trudge through this day with my heart feeling burdened with cares and woes. I have a choice. I have the power to find humor, beauty and human kindness in this day if I will look for them.

What I sometimes forget is that I am largely responsible for the quality of my daily life. If I wait for the pleasant things in life to come to me, they will come from time to time. But I do not have to wait passively for my good. I can make plans to create happy and satisfying experiences today even if it is in small ways. I can look for beauty and joy today. I believe I will try.

I have always suspected the quality of my recovery will dictate how long it lasts. If it only is pain and struggle for no purpose, no happiness, why should I bother?

Today, I will create a positive experience for myself. I will embrace every difficulty for the lesson it brings.

Nothing is a waste of time if you
use the experience wisely.
—AUGUSTE RODIN

L ike other addicts, I tend to be very tough on myself. When I
found out how crabby I was without nicotine, I started using it
again. There is a twisted logic in that for me.

I expected a period of being short-tempered during withdrawal. But
even when I no longer had severe cravings, I still found myself angry.
"Working the Steps" with my sponsor, I learned that I still have
unresolved anger issues to work through.

Anger is a sign of a lesson to be learned. When I was using nicotine
to drug my feelings, I never examined them and never learned how to
deal with them. Now anger shows me I have a problem to solve.

I used to think I had to be perfect, or at least not let others see my
imperfections. I needed to be emotionally cool so others could not take
advantage of me. It is not always easy to admit I am not in control and
that I am very human.

As I work the Program, I am learning all humans are imperfect. I
have individual strengths and weakness. Step Four and Step Five help me
see that the weaknesses of which I am most ashamed are frequently
character traits that are out of balance. I find that I have strengths that
help me balance my weaknesses.

*Today, I embrace all my traits. That helps me recognize
and appreciate the positive in others.*

Bear in mind, for your comfort, that we only
perceive our malady when the cure begins.
—ARCHBISHOP FRANÇOIS FÉNELON

A long the coastline is a stand of trees that I love to see. The steady wind from the ocean has twisted, turned and stunted those trees into fantastic shapes.

My habits have the same powerful effect on me. The constant, steady repeating of the same choices made me the person I am. Some of those habits are good and important to my happiness. Other choices I now choose to reject now that I can see their effect on me. How lucky I am to have seen the effect of my nicotine addiction. I needed strength to make a new choice when the old urge prompted me to use.

My Higher Power and members of Nicotine Anonymous give me the support I need to continue growing in healthier directions. I am free to study the twists and stunted growth my addiction created. Then I discover ways of nurturing those parts of my personality into healthy new growth.

Today, I am grateful to find new ways of
dealing with my personality and life.

A people that values its privileges above its
principles soon loses both.
—DWIGHT D. EISENHOWER

Service has always been an important concept in Twelve Step
Programs. Many Nicotine Anonymous meetings do not have a
coffee break with snacks. As a result, the first visible sign of service,
helping by making coffee, is missing. That is OK, since coffee is a
problem for many of us who wish to stay free of nicotine. I found I
could not have coffee for a long time because it triggered cravings for
nicotine.

There are still many ways to serve. I can put out literature or order
it. I can chair a meeting. I can welcome newcomers. I can talk with
struggling members on the phone. I can maintain the phone list. I can
bring a cake to celebrate another member's birthday, even my own. I can
participate in group conscious meetings.

The most important service I can provide is to share my "experience,
strength and hope" with the addict who still suffers. That is what this
Program is about. From the beginning Twelve Step Programs have
understood that "service is the key" to recovery.

Today, I will find a way to help another person.

JULY 19

Live your life as you see fit. That's not selfish. Selfish is
to demand that others live their lives as you see fit.
—ANTHONY DE MELLO

As I think back to my smoking days, I remember how selfish I
was. When a group of us went out to dinner, it did not matter
how many did not smoke. What mattered is that I smoked, and
we better sit in the smoking section. I was not considerate at all of how
they felt, or what they needed. I knew that at some point in the dinner, I
was going to need a cigarette. I can just picture myself trying to get in the
door first, so I could tell the hostess we needed the smoking section.

Now, I find myself being angry when a member in my group wants
to sit in the smoking section. I am a nonsmoker, and they should respect
that. At least that is the way I felt at the beginning. Now, I realize that if I
can be a good example to them, they may want to join the nonsmoking
people in this world.

When the Program was new to me, I had to set limits. Now, I just
ask my Higher Power to guide me through difficult situations. I am
learning to see the world without the smoke screen clouding my vision.
Every day, I look for areas of my life that I have not seen yet. It is
wonderful.

*Today, I will look at the way I see people who are
different. Do I accept them just as they are?*

Good company in a journey
makes the way seem shorter.

—IZAAK WALTON

When I came to Nicotine Anonymous, I had three years in Alcoholics Anonymous. Early in my recovery from alcohol I discovered that cigarettes made it easier not to drink. I traded my alcohol addiction for an even greater reliance on nicotine.

In the Nicotine Anonymous Fellowship, I learned that I could truly count on fellow members to help me through the most painful separation from my Savior nicotine. In that separation process I learned that letting go of nicotine was the real deal. I did not have any powerful substitute substances to replace nicotine. It was now truly to be "life on life's terms."

I came to see that my recovery up until that point was profoundly limited by my incessant nicotine use.

Today, I am learning, finally, to live life.
I no longer hide from life.

Make up your mind to act decidedly and take
the consequences. No good is ever done
in this world by hesitating.
—THOMAS HENRY HUXLEY

L ike many others, I put off attempting to do anything about my
nicotine addiction for years. I heard about things I could try;
witnessed others who were able to stop. But I hesitated, "not yet,
maybe someday." These words became all too familiar.

Hesitation can make an eternity out of a pause. Setting life on hold is
part of my pattern. I often lit up as a means to create a pause. I wanted to
hold off the outside world or stuff my inside world.

Recovery encourages me to act decidedly and to accept the
consequences. This is being alive. Hesitation is like holding my breath; it
approaches death. Each time I decide to act and accept the results, I am in
the flow of life and therefore connected to its energy.

*Today, cleared of the fog of addiction, I can respond consciously to
my circumstances and be invigorated by this engagement.*

I'm passionately involved in life: I love its change, its color, its
movement. To be alive, to be able to see, to walk, to have
houses, music, paintings—it's all a miracle.
—ARTHUR RUBINSTEIN

When I was using nicotine I always had the sense that life was passing me by. It never occurred to me that this might be connected to my total subservience to my addiction. Today I feel fully enrolled in my life. It is the feeling that I am no longer squandering God's greatest gift, life.

*Today I celebrate freedom free from the bondage of
nicotine addiction. I have been reborn.*

> You can always tell a real friend: when you've
> made a fool of yourself he doesn't feel you've
> done a permanent job.
> —LAURENCE J. PETER

I will always remember my first meeting and the way I felt when I was greeted with the word, "Welcome." I was afraid of going to my first meeting, afraid of connecting with people who did not use nicotine, and afraid of facing my addiction. That sincere welcome was just what I needed.

Going to meetings and becoming a member of the Fellowship of Nicotine Anonymous has helped me to stay nicotine-free for nearly five years. The love and acceptance I have received has freed me from the isolation I once lived in. I was never able to truly be a "part of" when I was still using nicotine.

I look forward to seeing my friends and fellow recovering nicotine addicts at meetings and sharing a special bond and understanding with them.

Today I know no matter what is going on in my life, I am always welcome at a Nicotine Anonymous meeting and can be a part of the Fellowship.

Let us be silent, that we may hear
the whispers of the gods.

—RALPH WALDO EMERSON

I have so many things on my mind. It goes in circles; it goes on tangents. That is the way my addict brain works.

My serenity comes back when I remember to focus. When I first started coming to meetings, my mind would slip off into making shopping lists. I would have to pull it back, rein it in. I told myself that for one hour I would focus on my recovery.

My ability to focus improved and keeps growing. Focus on my recovery is how I stay in recovery. I remind myself all the time that my recovery, staying clean and continuing to grow, is the most important thing in my life.

Today, I will be fully present during meetings. If my mind wanders I will bring it back.

The most utterly lost of all days, is that in
which you have not once laughed.

—CHAMFORT (NEE SÉBASTIEN ROCH NICOLAS)

I t was time, time to take that break. The first fifteen-minute break of
the forty-hour work week on Monday morning. I was anticipating
meeting my friend and I knew that he was smoking. I gave him my
pack.

"Would you take these" I said, "and smoke them for me?"

"Okay," he said, "thanks."

We were standing around the parking lot and I was thinking about
what to do while he smokes. I needed to laugh. I took a mouthful of
water and gargled. Then I pretended to be an elephant.

Soon we were laughing.

Today, I will take time to laugh and enjoy life.

I have sworn upon the altar of God,
eternal hostility against every form of
tyranny over the mind of man.
—THOMAS JEFFERSON

This country's history is interwoven with the institution of slavery. Very early, some of the colonies realized how valuable a cash crop tobacco was, and how important slave labor was to grow and produce it.

Slavery was abolished in the U.S. in 1863, but it still exists for those of us addicted to nicotine. Through the Fellowship of the Program I can remain free of the bondage of nicotine.

*Today, I know I can only live free if I am
free from practicing my addiction.*

The whole purpose of creation is to give form to Divine
Love. Do we wake up every morning, excited to get to
be Divine Love in expression?

—REV. DIANA HUGHES

C hronic low self-esteem went with my enslavement to nicotine for
many years prior to recovery. Following the shock of initial
withdrawal, the Fellowship provided a safe haven to process the
myriad and at times confusing array of new feelings and emotions that
surfaced in those first weeks. Eventually, manageability around anger and
higher energy left me feeling much better about myself. This took some
getting used to.

Today when I feel confused or driven, I ask what it is I am enslaved
to. If I still struggle I pause again, asking my Higher Power for self-
honesty. Am I taking myself too seriously? Am I entertaining a spirit of
superiority in my personal relations? Am I hungry? Although the gift of
insight may guide me, am I deferring to God's timetable?

Accepting my limitations, God's will might simply be the next thing.
If my mind is ahead of the task, I try to come back to the present. If that
is too much, maybe I need a rest, a talk with a friend, some quiet time.

---

*Today, situations need not overcome me. With
help, I can be in the moment, free to choose
without fuss or confusion.*

Dream manfully and nobly,
and thy dreams shall be prophets.

—EDWARD BULWER-LYTTON

I really dreaded taking Step Four and Step Five. What a surprise to discover that I am no worse than anyone else. I learned that any character defect is simply an imbalance. For every weakness, I found a corresponding strength. I no longer have to fear examining my weaknesses because I know I will find strengths.

I continue to find that I am free to do things that I previously envied. I have faith that envious thoughts are simply God's way of letting me know I can open myself to receive. Whenever I envy another's accomplishments, I discover a dream of my own. Incredibly, whenever I acknowledge the dream and claim it, I find no difficulty in achieving that dream.

Truly God does give us envy to show us our own possibilities. Embraced appropriately, envy is not a monster, but a gift. No one has to have less for me to claim my dreams.

*Today, I know with the support of my
friends no dream is beyond reach.*

Just as despair can come to one only from other
human beings, hope, too, can be given to one only
by other human beings.

—ELIE WEISEL

O nce at a meeting, I heard another member mention how many
times he estimated he had used nicotine. That made me curious.
I did my own calculations. I discovered that eighty percent of
my nicotine consumption was after I made the rational decision to quit,
and did quit for eleven months. I discovered that sixty percent of my
nicotine consumption was after part of my left lung was removed.

I was a teenager when the surgeon general first mandated nicotine
warnings. Like my friends, I was not concerned. The dangers were for
those who consumed a lot of nicotine. We were sure we would not be
more than casual users.

Actually, even then I suspected I might. I would not tell my friends
how important nicotine was to me, how a craved it, how I went to great
lengths to use it.

From the first time I quit, then had one hit and could not stop, I
knew I was addicted. My excuse was always that I would quit if I could.
I just always thought my addiction was more powerful than others. Then
I came to Nicotine Anonymous, and found others whose addictions
were equally strong. Only, they were living without nicotine and they
were happy. They gave me the hope I desperately needed.

Today, I thank God for directing me to
Nicotine Anonymous and freedom.

Unbeing dead isn't being alive.
—e. e. cummings

When I was still hopelessly chained to my nicotine addiction, I tried every method to quit. It was hopeless. I knew I was addicted emotionally, mentally, and physically to the nicotine and to the habit. I had a strong need for oral gratification.

It was the oral gratification that scared me the most. I did not quit secretly sucking my thumb when I needed comfort until I started using nicotine. Mine was not a thirty-plus year addiction, it was based on a life-long addiction. Nicotine not only provided the oral gratification, it actually medicated my feelings.

With nicotine I could be energized or calm down. I did not have to deal with painful feelings. I could isolate or belong. I could be visible or invisible. Best of all, I could always control the outcome. I knew people with addictions to drugs or alcohol. They could not control the result.

I was petrified of living without nicotine. I did not believe it would be possible. Then I found Nicotine Anonymous. I listened to others share their stories, and I came to believe it would be possible to live without my drug and habit.

Today, I will deal with my feelings,
not stuff or medicate them.

Only a few things are really important.
—MARIE DRESSLER

I have always loved to read. I frequently use reading to escape from uncomfortable reality. As a young child, I would lie in bed and read from the light of a street lamp. I have been known to stay up all night to finish a good book.

Early in my recovery, I found I could not concentrate and stay awake to read more than a few pages at a time. I found that I could not stay focused on difficult tasks. I was worried that I would never regain my lost concentration.

In meetings, I heard others talk about their own lack of concentration. They eventually regained their former level of focus. So did I.

I also have learned to take breaks when I am having a problem in focusing. I have learned that my concentration suffers the most when I am doing a task that I do not like. I discovered that I had used nicotine to force myself to do tasks that I did not enjoy because others needed me or expected me to accomplish those tasks.

Today, I am free to accept tasks that fulfill me instead of forcing myself to accommodate others needs.

AUGUST 1

Any idiot can face a crisis—it's day-to-day living
that wears you out.
—ANTON CHEKHOV

I have a severe addiction to nicotine. At meetings I found hope. I promised myself that I would give my recovery my absolute highest priority. One of the ways I proved that was by attending every meeting unless I was out of town.

I was on my way to a Saturday noon meeting. I was pulling out, turning right, into a six-lane divided street. I barely glanced to my right since no traffic could be coming from that direction. I was watching to my left for a break in traffic. When there was a break, I took my foot off the brake. I immediately felt a bump and heard someone screaming. I hit the brakes and turned my head. I discovered, to my horror, that I had hit a pedestrian.

She was knocked down, bruised and had a scraped knee, but because I had not even touched the accelerator, she was not seriously injured. She refused medical attention, but agreed to let me drive her home.

I affirmed that nicotine was "not an option" as I drove on to the meeting. By the end of the meeting, I had calmed down. As I drove away, I had a surge of confidence. I no longer was craving nicotine. I knew if I could get through that, it would take something really big to make me cave in.

I keep going to meetings to remember how life used to be for me. Otherwise, I forget I am a nicotine addict.

---

*Today, I am confident I can deal with any
event as long as I practice my Program.*

> You, yourself, as much as anybody in the entire
> universe, deserve your love and affection.
> —BUDDHA

I used nicotine to stuff my feelings. I never felt as though I belonged. I always felt I had to continuously justify my existence. I devoted enormous effort and energy to being the person others expected me to be. No task was beneath me. No effort too great

I was a single mom, working sixty hours a week, taking two or three graduate level courses each semester, devoting at least an hour each night to quality time with my child. How? I used to get up at 4:00 a.m. to study, and I would get to bed about midnight.

For years I never read anything except texts or work materials. I never did anything for fun for myself. I played games with my child, but I did not have time for myself. Everyone else's needs took precedence over mine. I did not take vacations. I bought my clothes at second-hand stores. I lived in the future. I was always working for a better life later.

In meetings I learned about boundaries. I had no concept of boundaries. First I had to learn what they are. Then I could work on figuring out my boundaries. Then I could work on enforcing them. Then I could define and enforce them without guilt.

Today, I will "stay in the present," and I will
give my needs the priority I deserve.

The deepest need of man is the need to overcome his
separateness, to leave the prison of his aloneness.
—ERICH FROMM

Peer pressure, the loneliness of low self-esteem, and the sexual enticement alluded to in movies all played a part in my early encounters with using nicotine. As a young person I was trying to develop an identity and a relationship with the world. Like others, I did this awkwardly, often foolishly, sometimes even desperately.

A youth wants to be somebody important enough to have a connection with a group. To be denied this is painful, a living death to some. With the focus on tobacco instead of my insecure self, I could bond more easily with my peers. It was: light up and be let in.

One of the strengths of a recovery program is that each member is important and useful. There is a bonding through the courage to show up. With sharing, the bond grows. Those still using nicotine keep the danger fresh for those who have put the drug down. Those who are clean offer hope to those who aspire. Recovery becomes our new connection. We bond in celebrating our dream, living free of nicotine.

*Today, any sense of aloneness is
comforted by a Fellowship of support
and contact with a Higher Power.*

Nothing will work unless you do.

—MAYA ANGELOU

Getting into service was easy for me since many of the members of my home group were involved within the group, with intergroup, or with World Services.

The first thing I did was to volunteer as my group's refreshment person, followed shortly as secretary, then intergroup representative. I eventually held several different positions for intergroup.

I noticed shortly after my first service position that my cravings lessened and sometime thereafter totally disappeared. I definitely feel this was a result of the amount of service I was willing and able to give.

Today, I know that service is something
I do for myself; if I help others in the
process that is an extra reward.

By three methods we may learn wisdom:
First, by reflection, which is noblest; second,
by imitation, which is easiest; and third by
experience, which is the bitterest.

—CONFUCIUS

Using nicotine started easy as pie. It was just a few a day because that was what my closest friend was doing. Peer pressure, but it did not seem that there was pressure at the time. It was easy except for the bad cough on that first one, and that was how it started. Just one and I was hooked, and it got progressively worse over the years.

Over the thirty-some years I had been smoking, I really had no idea why I smoked other than just being a habit. I would have one at the top of every hour just like clockwork. I had a really hard time passing up that first one in the morning even before my feet hit the ground.

Today I have come to hate nicotine, and the fact that I was a victim to nicotine for so long. I pray my healing continues, and I never run into worse health problems because of my past history of addiction.

There is no logic behind using nicotine, it had just become habit, but there are tons of logic behind what I am doing about it. Now I am very proud of myself, and I feel I have more backbone than ever before. I truly am living life more abundantly as a direct result of this Twelve Step Program.

*Today, if I find myself attracted to nicotine I will
remind myself that nicotine is not my friend.*

AUGUST 6

I put my hand in God's and God takes care of
everything (if I don't get in the way).
—NICOTINE ANONYMOUS: THE BOOK

I had quit smoking at age forty-two, having smoked since age eleven. My father had died of lung cancer, my sister died of cancer, my mother of emphysema. They all smoked until they died. At age forty-nine, it seemed like a good idea to have a cigar with the boys after dinner one night. Within two weeks I was hooked again.

I am a health care practitioner and had to resort to all the old hiding and sneaking behavior I learned smoking in school. After a time I knew I had to quit so I began going to this Nicotine Anonymous meeting near my office on Monday nights.

I went to meetings consistently for two years and eleven months before I got my first twenty-four hour chip. For two years and eleven months, in the throes of self-loathing and addiction, I went to bed every night convinced that would be my last day to smoke. By eight o'clock the next morning I had dug the smokes out of the trash, picked the butts up off the yard, or microwaved the cigarettes I had run water over the night before.

I was certain that I had the willpower to kick this nasty habit. It was only when I gave up my self-will and surrendered to my Higher Power that the obsession was removed. It is now eighteen months since I have smoked. I go to meetings and gratefully pray regularly.

Today, I am willing to be willing, to follow the Steps, to
do the footwork, and to leave everything else up to God.
I breathe deeply and exhale easily.

Life is a succession of lessons that must
be lived to be understood.
—THOMAS CARLYLE

It was icy as I drove home from work. With three months nicotine-free, my nerves were as raw as hamburger meat. I was driving in snow and my knuckles were white gripping the steering wheel. The car in front of me slid into the intersection through a red light. I slid neatly behind him just short of hitting his bumper. Then I felt a gigantic bang into the back of my car; the vehicle behind me slid into my car. My neck snapped and I felt my insides shift from back to front. I sat dazed staring at the snowflakes. Had I just been in an accident? It seemed like a movie script.

The man in the other car jumped out and walked toward my car. I stepped out gingerly, afraid of what to expect. My car bumper was scratched but still in place.

The man immediately inquired about my condition.

"Are you all right?" he said.

I said yes, and immediately asked him for a cigarette, not if he was hurt, or if his car was damaged. Thankfully, he did not have any. This is the mind of a nicotine addict.

Fortunately I found Nicotine Anonymous and I celebrated my fifth nicotine-free anniversary in 2004. Now, when I drive home on the ice, I chew gum and play the radio really loud. Lots of awful things have happened since I quit and I have suffered lots of stress but the one thing I do not have to suffer with anymore is being an active nicotine addict.

Today, I am grateful to manage stress without having to resort to using nicotine.

> Don't go around saying the world
> owes you a living. The world owes you
> nothing. It was here first.
>
> —MARK TWAIN

I am a victim. Or at least in my mind I have been a victim. As children we are helpless and not able to control our circumstances. But some of us continue to believe this into our adult life. For me it has been a way of life.

I did not realize I was harming myself or my relationships. I did not know I could live another way. I stood behind my veil of nicotine, blaming others for things that happened to me. I only wanted to see what was wrong with my life. I was not willing to look for the miracles in life.

Then I started hearing in my Nicotine Anonymous meetings about sitting on the "pity pot." I heard about gratitude, being grateful for what I have. I also heard that I could not be resentful and grateful at the same time. I heard that by giving up being a victim I could be free. I realized that I could be grateful if I did not see myself as a victim. Now with the help of other nicotine addicts I am able to see something wonderful and joyful in my life because I am willing to look for it.

Today, I will not give up my power by thinking like a victim; I will remember that I always have choices.

Shoot for the moon. If you miss
you will land with the stars.
—MARY KAY ASH

I used to suffer from the delusion that I was more addicted than others. I would quit using nicotine, but my addiction was simply too strong. Then I found Nicotine Anonymous.

At my first meeting, I was amazed to hear people who seemed to be enjoying life without nicotine. Then across the room from me, another member shared part of his story. He was clearly as addicted as I was, but he had not used nicotine in two months.

For the first time, I found hope that even I could learn to live comfortably and happily without nicotine.

*Today, I know nothing is impossible because
I can find and accept all the support I need to
accomplish every dream.*

No matter what our specific religious beliefs may have been
or are, participation in Nicotine Anonymous and
concentration on the Twelve Steps has led us to realize that
there is a Power greater than ourselves.

—NICOTINE ANONYMOUS: THE BOOK

When I started using nicotine at age eleven, I also began learning how to lie, steal and sneak.

When my Grandma told me it would stunt my growth I did not believe her. There seemed to be plenty of big people who used nicotine. I did not then know about emotional growth.

By beginning a life of defiance and secrecy from my parents I also gave up the only Higher Power I knew. I was on my own. Along with nicotine, I had to learn to hide my fear and most all other emotions, at first from others, ultimately from myself.

My admission of powerlessness was my first opening for my Higher Power to become available to me. What a relief. Without nicotine, I am learning to walk through the day-to-day joys and griefs of life without hiding, denying or stuffing my feelings. My Higher Power and the Fellowship of the meetings are there to walk with me. I am able now to completely exhale.

*Today, my Higher Power is doing for
me what I cannot do for myself.*

Success seems to be largely a matter of
hanging on after others have let go.
—WILLIAM FEATHER

I started using nicotine because I did not know how to handle my emotions, and because I was uncomfortable in social situations. It was not long before using nicotine became my response to any emotion or situation. Nicotine was my crutch whenever I was happy, sad, angry, hungry, lonely, tired, excited, when I felt anything. I used at home, at work, on vacations, before job interviews, in the shower, anywhere. I tried to stop, but the thought of stopping terrified me. One morning, as my heart was racing with panic because I had no supply, I thought, "Wow, it's freezing outside. I look awful, and I am going to the store right now. That is true dedication. If only I could apply this same kind of dedication to quitting, I could quit."

What a revelation. Then, a voice inside my head said, "That's not dedication, that's addiction." In that moment, I realized I was truly powerless over nicotine. I still went to the store and bought my nicotine, but the seed of truth had been planted. A few months later, I was in a Nicotine Anonymous meeting getting my first chip. That was over a year ago, and I am still powerless over nicotine, but I am gratefully nicotine-free.

*Today, I remember one is too many, and a
thousand will never be enough.*

Patience with others is Love; Patience with self is
Hope; Patience with God is Faith.
—ADEL BESTAVROS

Nicotine was the friend who never let me down. It was always there whenever I needed it, whether I liked it or not. You see, the real truth was that nicotine was in control.

My friend had taken me hostage. How could I ever break free?

For me, the biggest step toward breaking free and remaining free is letting go. Letting go is not giving up. It is giving away. When I have a craving, I imagine that I am holding the craving in my hands. It is a small, green, ugly creature. I hold my hands up to God, and I say, "Please take this from me. I don't want it anymore. Thanks." Then, I take a deep breath and another and another until the craving goes away. To me, this is what "let go and let God" means.

Letting go was and is difficult for me. I am learning to live my life free of nicotine "one day at a time." I could not do it without the help of others who understand my struggle and pain, or without a Higher Power who is my true, and now thankfully not my only, friend.

Today, I realize "the craving will pass,"
whether or not I use nicotine.

Hope begins in the dark; the stubborn hope that if you just
show up and try to do the right thing, the dawn will come.
You wait and watch and work: you don't give up.

—ANNE LAMOTT

Some time ago my husband made me really mad. The old me may
have walked away, but "working the Steps" has taught me to focus
on only my part.

I had to ask myself if I wanted to end our relationship, and the
answer was no. To continue the relationship I would have to let go of my
anger some time, so why not now? Next I could look at what the result
would be if I surrendered. I was not in any danger; I did not have to
compromise the truth. I made the decision to accept his position as an act
of love.

Once I turned the situation around and saw that I could give him a
gift, I felt good about myself. Once I felt whole, I discovered my anger
had disappeared.

*Today, I will let go of my need
to be right and choose love.*

The future belongs to those who
believe in the beauty of their dreams.
—ELEANOR ROOSEVELT

I struggled for more than twenty years to be comfortable living life without nicotine. My struggle ended when I found Nicotine Anonymous.

I was scared it would not work and I was equally scared it would work. I simply could not imagine living without nicotine. My first year of recovery was incredible. Rather than suffer the upheaval of anger, I experienced rainbows.

Every day for the first year I saw a rainbow, sometimes natural ones, but more often man-made ones. Once I even saw a triple rainbow. Another time, I was really irritated by a driver who cut in front of me to make a sudden exit from the freeway, only to see that he had a rainbow hanging from his rear view mirror.

Where were all those rainbows before recovery? Most likely they were all around me, but I was too isolated from reality to see them.

*Today, I will be present to the
simple pleasures life offers.*

I have friends in overalls whose friendship I would
not swap for the favor of the kings of the world.
—THOMAS A. EDISON

There is no we without me. I used to think that I smoked cigarettes alone. I found out, by coming to Nicotine Anonymous meetings for support, that I need people. I needed others to grow tobacco. I needed all the people who processed it into my chosen delivery system. I was obsessed and addicted to nicotine for forty years. I needed people to get money to pay for my addiction and to clean up after my mess.

I prayed for help. The answer was for me to start a Nicotine Anonymous group. Initially I still used nicotine. I found I need people to get clean and to live "one day at a time." I will have a longer, healthier life. Only by living can there be a we.

*Today, I will support those who struggle, and
I will accept support for my difficulties.*

AUGUST 16

Life consists not in holding good cards but in
playing those you hold well.
—JOSH BILLINGS

There are days when I must deal with life on its terms, not as I would like my life or day to turn out. Acceptance comes harder when I believe that my way is the best and only way. When my life or day does not go as planned, I usually tend to either analyze it to death, or try to fix or change the situation. All of these actions create mental and emotional stress and turmoil, and ultimately affect my spirituality and serenity. My best choice is to accept that everything happens for a reason, and that my Higher Power has a plan that will exceed my expectations if I just sit back and let it happen.

I know my Higher Power is leading me Step-by-Step to the highest good, and to the best answers to my prayers and desires of my heart.

*Today, my faith in my Higher Power
is greater than any challenge.*

Life is half spent before we know what it is.

—GEORGE HERBERT

Starting in the eighth grade, I went to boarding school. That meant that a few times each year I would be unsupervised on a bus for long hours. I would always buy a pack of cigarettes for the trip.

I did not want to look like an inexperienced kid, so I watched the other smokers on the bus. I would have one, and almost immediately want to light up, but I would wait until someone else lit another. Because I did not want to look as though I were copying, I would wait a few more minutes.

At that point, I was a binge smoker. I could not smoke freely, but I took advantage of situations when I was alone.

Looking back, I can see clearly that I spent my life waiting to indulge my nicotine addiction. I ended my nicotine career isolating so that I was never separated from my drug. And I never had enough.

Today, I embrace life; I no longer
waste my time waiting.

> One of the most tragic things I know about
> human nature is that all of us tend to put off
> living. We are all dreaming of some magical
> rose garden over the horizon.
>
> —DALE CARNEGIE

Toward the end of my nicotine career, they banned smoking in the office, and I joined the all-weather addicts.

After suffering all day, all I wanted to do when I went home was to indulge my addiction. I would sit in my blue chair and light one after another. Eventually I would know I needed to start dinner for my family, and I would promise myself I would after just one more.

I found myself grieving the separation from nicotine. I would light a cigarette while promising to fix dinner after just this one more, and I could already feel the pain. I was totally isolated. I would not allow anyone or anything to come between my drug and me in my non-working hours.

Then I was directed to Nicotine Anonymous and you helped me on the road to recovery.

Today, I am free to be with
others and enjoy life.

It makes no sense to worry about things you have no control
over because there's nothing you can do about them, and why
worry about things you do control?

—MOTHER TERESA

I struggled for twenty years to live without nicotine. One time I had
quit for a few weeks and was starting to feel good about myself. Then
I had a stressful day at work.

We had major crisis with a customer. My boss was traveling the
globe to find a solution, and I was stuck in the office unable to do
anything other than pass information around and arrange conference
calls.

I started feeling tightness in my chest and tingling in my left arm. I
thought about the possibility of a heart attack, but there was no way I
would desert my post. I tried walking up and down stairs to relieve the
tension, but that did not work. Finally I caved in, and left the office long
enough to buy and indulge in my drug.

Nicotine Anonymous helped free me from my life as a crisis junkie.

*Today, I will face life's challenges and
celebrations with a clear mind.*

Loving people live in a loving world;
hostile people live in a hostile world.
Same world. How come?

—DR. WAYNE W. DYER

Today, I realized that my world is changing. I am changing. I am making choices that will make my life better than before. For over forty years, I have hidden behind a smoke screen. I was afraid to see the world, or to let the world see the real me.

I now realize that I used cigarettes to hide my true feelings. When I was in a difficult situation, and did not want to face the facts, I would stall and take a drag on my cigarette. I would use that puff of smoke to hide behind. I never thought of how many times a day I used nicotine to stuff my true feelings.

I am now learning that there are many ways that I can deal with the world without killing myself in the process. I can just take a deep breath before I answer a question. I can also take a quick walk when I am feeling depressed, instead of hiding my frustrations behind a cloud of smoke.

This is a whole new way of life for me. I am starting to see the world and all the beauty that has been given to me. I am finally able to see the wonder of the world as my Higher Power had intended. I find joy in seeing at least one new thing of beauty each and every day. I am so grateful.

Today I choose to see beauty in the world. I choose
to see the love and assistance that my Higher
Power is providing for me each day.

> How do you do? You do by learning. And, how
> do you learn? You learn by doing.
>
> —PETER MCWILLIAMS

I have been learning new things constantly, since I quit smoking. One of the things that especially caught my attention was the fact that smokers inhale deeply, and often. When I quit smoking, I learned one reason all the programs that aid a person in quitting suggested taking ten deep breaths when the cravings start. It is to imitate the way we used to inhale on a cigarette.

My problem was that I rarely thought of doing this exercise. And when I did do it, I felt silly. My mind would wander after about four breaths, and it did not seem to help curb my craving. At least, it did not help until I was at a Nicotine Anonymous meeting and someone shared the following meditation. It was suggested that with each inhale, I recite one line of this verse. If I repeated the verse twice, I would get the ten deep breaths. I found this very helpful, and I still use it when I feel tense in any situations.

Be still, and know that I am God.
Be still, and know that I am.
Be still, and know.
Be still.
Be.

When I use this meditation, I feel that my Higher Power is giving me the strength to overcome any problem that I am facing at the time.

---

*Today, I will meditate on these words
and be thankful for each breath.*

Everyone is too old for something, but
no one is too old for everything.
—GARSON KANIN

While I was still smoking, I found it difficult to do a lot of things. Some of the things I did not do were not even related to my age. I did not go to the theater, or a museum, or the library, or to other places that did not allow smoking.

Years ago, smoking was more acceptable. I can even remember when it was possible to request a smoking room in the hospital. Doctors and counselors would smoke with you. It is no wonder why I found it so difficult to understand the health hazards. It was like a complete turnaround in my brain. I fought the new statistics for years. I did not want to believe that things could have changed that much in my short lifetime.

Now, since I quit smoking, I not only enjoy going to nonsmoking buildings, but I also enjoy being out in nature. I can take long, wonderful walks in the parks or forest, and I know that I am not harming the environment with my smoking. I really have learned a lot since I quit smoking. I feel like a new spring flower that has just opened its petals to the world. I am also willing to try things that I did not want to try before, like t'ai chi, yoga, and singing out loud. There is an entire new world out there for me. I am loving every moment of my new life.

Today, I am eager to learn new things,
especially since I can now breathe.

*If you keep saying things are going to be bad, you
have a good chance of being a prophet.*
—ISAAC BASHEVIS SINGER

I never considered myself a prophet, however, there were times that I would fall into a negative mode. I would listen to people who told me that quitting is just about impossible. Others would say, "If you really want to quit, you should just throw the cigarettes away, and be done with them." I heard every comment imaginable. I even got advice from people who never smoked.

I had tried to quit many times: sometimes for a few hours; sometimes for a couple of days. The longest was three months. I started to believe these negative comments, because I had not yet learned about Nicotine Anonymous. I did not realize that a support group would make all the difference in the world for me. I could use any of the products that were on the market, but none of them could give me what I needed. I needed a support group, the Twelve Steps, and a Higher Power.

One of the slogans that helped me most, was "one day at a time." When I quit this time, I sat my family down, and said, "I do not know what will happen tomorrow, but today, I will not smoke." Every night before I went to sleep, my husband would say, "You got one more. I am so proud of you." Those words meant the world to me.

*Today, I thank my Higher Power for giving me people who knew
what they were talking about to guide me through the tough times.*

We realized that using nicotine was more than a
bad habit; rather, it was a symptom that our lives
were out of control and unmanageable. The
destructive aspects of our addiction went far
beyond the obvious damage we did to our bodies.

—NICOTINE ANONYMOUS: THE BOOK

The First Step is when we start to get honest, to be true to ourselves and admit the role nicotine played in our lives. It controlled virtually every aspect by determining our friends, how we performed our jobs, the restaurants we visited, who drove to events. Airplane trips were measured in how long we could go without a cigarette. We would dread long stretches at work where we would be without nicotine.

Before Step One is a more basic Step, one which we admitted years ago, but one which we just realized. It is Step zero and it says, "This has got to stop."

*Today, I realize I can begin anew
anytime I wish.*

Always bear in mind that your own
resolution to succeed is more important than
any other one thing.

—ABRAHAM LINCOLN

I really loved nicotine. There was nothing I would not do for it. All the while I fed my addiction I knew it was killing me. Literally, thousands and thousands of times I ingested nicotine to relieve my anxiety, or in celebration, knowing I was going to die. My attitude was acceptance of the fact that I was going to die still using it or from having used it. I had committed myself to the relationship 'til death do us part.

A few years ago, my friend Ted and I were discussing issues around love. He asked me, "Do you know what the opposite of love is?" "Of course," I replied, "hate." Ted then revealed to me a new awareness by explaining, "No, actually it is indifference."

That is the point that I reached with nicotine. Finally, after years of doing everything in my power to control it, I got a new attitude, an attitude of indifference. Nicotine could not hurt me any worse by not using it than it had by using it.

Today, I realize there is but one thing over which I have total control, and that is my attitude. I will aim for a positive attitude.

We awakened from that time of slow suicide by
nicotine use, when our spirits were devoured in a
vast ocean of self-loathing, smashed by endless
waves of craving, fear, and failure.
—NICOTINE ANONYMOUS: THE BOOK

When the fear of not quitting outweighed the fear of quitting, I
was ready to quit. Sometimes fear is defined as the opposite of
faith. I was told if I did not have the faith just yet, simply
believe that others had it. I absolutely could not stop on my own no
matter what method I tried. Just as absolutely, I could not have stopped
without the people in Nicotine Anonymous who had faith.

They had the faith that I could make it through each craving. They
said the craving would pass whether I lit up or not, and the first time I
rode it out I saw their faces. I had fear of facing them reporting I had
used nicotine, but I had lost my fear of failure. I gave up that fear with
the attitude of "Bring it on." It was not a defiant attitude, but one of
hopeful resignation. In meetings I found people who had made it
through the cravings, the fears, and the failures of past attempts. I learned
faith. At long last I was ready to face life.

*Today, I choose to live with faith,
facing life with my Higher Power.*

When I stand before God at the end of my life, I would
hope that I would not have a single bit of talent left, and
could say, "I used everything you gave me."

—ERMA BOMBECK

When I first started on my journey to recovery from nicotine addiction, I had a smaller life, a smaller world, and a smaller Higher Power.

My life was limited by where I could go when I used nicotine. For example, I could not go inside the door of a warm building to escape the bitter cold. My life was tied to my nicotine using partners and their schedules. I avoided people and places where nicotine use was not welcome.

Now I must admit that being inside the warm building was beyond my wildest dreams. Taking a twenty-four-hour flight to visit exotic places in the opposite side of the world was not imaginable.

Traveling is only one of many incredible experiences I have enjoyed because I am free from addiction and cravings.

Today, the excitement of a new world is mine
if I choose to be open to the experience.

Go to your bosom: knock there, and ask your
heart what it doth know.

—WILLIAM SHAKESPEARE

Almost every time I attend a meeting on Step Eleven, I begin by
saying it is my favorite Step. I would not have come to Nicotine
Anonymous if it were not for my own personal morning prayer.
At this point, I have a little over fourteen years off nicotine. I feel
like I would be incomplete without prayer and meditation. I pray in the
shower, in my car and all through the day. I also meditate actively during
as much of my day as I can. I just look and listen to see or hear messages
from my Higher Power that guide me to be the best I can be. Formal
prayer and meditation are the ways I search for God and find what God
has in store for me.

*Today, I will consciously seek my Higher Power to
discover the best life has to offer me.*

Oh Divine Master, grant that I may not so much
seek to be consoled, as to console; to be
understood, as to understand; to be loved, as to
love. For it is in giving that we receive.

—ST. FRANCIS OF ASSISI

I had been loved all of my life to the best ability of my family and
friends. But I never really let the love in. I did not come to Nicotine
Anonymous expecting to find love. I am sure that God has always
loved me. But I did not let God's love in much either. I was well guarded.

Meetings were consistently loving. I found that you listened to me.
You did not judge me. You hugged me, and encouraged me to "keep
coming back." As other members did these things for me, I began to
realize I could open up to accepting love. I also began to love you in all
the ways you had loved me. Finally, years into the process, I began to
love myself. Now I can look in the mirror and say, "I love you" and
mean it. Or I can sit quietly alone and know that I am loveable.

*Today, I know doing loving things for
others helps me become more loveable.*

My business is not to remake myself, but to make
the absolute best of what God made.
—ROBERT BROWNING

I do not believe man has infinite wisdom; that is why I leave all my
extreme challenges or impossibilities up to God. I delight in knowing
God's opportunities. When I was ready to give up, Nicotine
Anonymous renewed my hope.

Hope is spirit of the unknown, my human nature, my grasp of
the present. Skinning my lips on a tightly rolled tobacco stimulant/
depressant was craziness, sickness. Finally, in trying again to be free of
the drug I knew, I became aware of the impossibility of my solo efforts.

Because I still believed in God, it seemed as though, in some way, I
could come to respect myself. I grew up with no understanding of the
word respect, so the idea of self-respect immediately became a curiosity
that I could perhaps find. Group support and patience with myself led
me to find this illusive self-respect. My experience of God became
stronger as my feeling for myself became clearer.

*Today, I live in hope relying on my Higher
Power to support me in every situation.*

Say what you mean
but don't say it mean.

—NICOTINE ANONYMOUS MEMBER

Now that I'm finally off nicotine and have cleared the way in my life to make it free of smoke, I am prone to get self-righteous in my attitude about others' smoke. When that happens I will remind myself that I was an active nicotine addict not so long ago and will say what I need to say in a kind and compassionate manner. It is right for me to ask that my breathing space be free of smoke but I do not need to be mean about it. Self-righteous indignation is not an attractive characteristic in recovery.

So as I go out into this new day, I will remember how blessed I am to be a non-smoker, a recovering nicotine addict. When I am grateful it is hard to be hateful. So I go forward remembering that what I think and what I say changes the way I will experience this day. I will be kind in my thoughts, words and actions today.

*Today, I pray for compassion and thank God
that I am "happy, joyous and free."*

> If you take responsibility for yourself you will
> develop a hunger to accomplish your dreams.
>
> —LES BROWN

I feel like smoking, but for this second, for this minute, for this hour, for this day, I do not want to smoke.

When I think about feeding my addiction, or when the cravings pop up, I would meditate on this mantra. If that did not work, I would recite it no matter where I was. This helped me stay away from feeding my addiction. I also go to meetings every week, and share my mantra with the group.

Today, I will take time to
use the tools of my Program.

The rose does best as a rose.
Lilies make the best lilies.
And look! You!
The best you around.
—BRUSH DANCE

When I do the Steps one of the things I cannot help but learn is my own uniqueness. Originally I was delinquent by listing only my defects. I learned to also list my strengths and assets. When I share my "experience, strength and hope" in meetings I am sharing my essence, and there is usually at least one person who will be touched by what I share. What a gift. Part of my healing from addiction is to begin to love myself.

*Today, I will appreciate my own uniqueness and
assets, knowing that they are a gift to share.*

I've learned that people will forget what you said,
people will forget what you did, but people will never
forget how you made them feel.

—MAYA ANGELOU

How true. We are so busy worrying about ourselves: did we say or do the right thing? If you want to worry about this, you will never have time to be concerned about anyone but yourself. Only when we truly give of ourselves, our time, our presence, our responsiveness, can we produce the lasting memory. Those are the true gifts: the gift of reaching out in love and self-forgetfulness.

*Today, I will try to give something of
myself to someone who is suffering.*

When it is dark enough,
you can see the stars.

—RALPH WALDO EMERSON

I used to fall into a litany of self-blame and negativity. If something went wrong, I believed that I deserved it, that somehow I was being punished for some wrong I had done.

Now I am learning that sometimes things happen that I cannot control and it is okay. I do not need to medicate away my sadness or the misfortune I have suffered. Instead I begin to look for the stars. What is a positive result of this event? And my mood shifts and life does not seem quite as hard as I was making it. I am so glad that I do not need to smoke today.

Today, when things seem darkest,
I will look for the positive side.

SEPTEMBER 5

How poor are they that have not patience!
—WILLIAM SHAKESPEARE

I was standing in line in the grocery store. It was the world's worst line. In front of me was a crazy person fumbling with his wallet, who could not figure out the change; the cashier was going nuts. After a long commotion, I finally came up to pay for my items. I was undisturbed and peaceful. The cashier stared at me. She thought I was a saint. "Wow," she said. She was shocked at my calm. She did not know my mother lay dying of cancer, waiting to die for seven months. I visited her every day. This inconvenience of waiting in line did not really add up to much. And it was, at that moment in time, the least of my worries.

Today, I will remember how impatient I was to have my next nicotine fix and be glad that I can wait a little longer.

Absorbing information is like walking in dew:
eventually you get wet.

—WANDA HENNIG

When I heard this phrase, it struck me that this is why I go to meetings and why going to meetings eventually works. I have seen many people appear and disappear from my regular meeting. The ones who stay are the ones that I see finally let go of nicotine. The strength of the Program is to "keep coming back." Eventually, you get wet.

Today, my prayer is for the nicotine addict who still suffers. I will reach out to help get him or her to a meeting.

The pursuit of Perfection often
impedes progress.
—GEORGE WILL

I get busy. I push. I talk a lot. I spend an exorbitant amount of time on the computer or the telephone. I forget to eat or I eat too much. I sleep a lot or not enough. I get short fused and aggressive or meek and passive. I do not exercise. I consume excess sugar and caffeine.

I get into this duality: this high-low, black-white, meek or wild state of mind. I forget that I just quit using nicotine and that my body and mind is detoxifying from all the chemicals and poisons that I ingested on a daily hourly basis.

When I am reminded that I recently quit by my sponsor, my Nicotine Anonymous group or my friends, I remember to lighten up and relax. I remember the slogan "let go and let God" and again allow my Higher Power to take care of the details and me. I start back at the first Three Steps. I am powerless. There is a Power greater than myself and I made a decision to turn my will and my life over to my Higher Power.

*Today, I may start acting compulsively, but I am
open to reminders to "let go and let God."*

> It is not the world we live in that counts; it is the
> way we live in the world that is important.
>
> —MANLY P. HALL

There are many people places and things that set off relay switches in my nervous system memories. Second-hand smoke is one of those for me.

After months of feeling stuck in the fear of being enticed by second-hand smoke, my Higher Power's wisdom finally dawned on me. Obsessing about the fear is unnecessary. Just because I am faced with a memory of when I was smoking, does not mean I have to smoke, or that I have to obsess about it.

My addiction would like me to believe that I will go back to the slavery and death of smoking if I am around second-hand smoke. But, that is not true. While I do not want to be around noxious smoke, sometimes it is hard to avoid. Since I am learning that I cannot control everything, acceptance seems key here.

I realize that there is a whole Fellowship of people in Nicotine Anonymous who have not gone back to the deadly grip of smoking just because they have been around second-hand smoke. I remember that I have a sponsor who is free, as well as many Nicotine Anonymous mentors and friends who are all free, "one day at a time." Hundreds of Nicotine Anonymous members who are breathing free cannot be wrong.

Today, I will say the Serenity Prayer
and feel compassion for others.

Not forever can one enjoy stillness and peace. But
misfortune and destruction are not final. When the
grass has been burnt by the fire of the steppe, it
will grow again in summer.
—WISDOM OF THE MONGOLIAN STEPPE

Quitting smoking for me was as if I had walked through a door.
One day I got it. I had smoked a pack a day for sixteen years
and one day at 11:00 a.m. I decided not to smoke. Just to see,
just to try. I felt like God was tapping me on the shoulder,
saying to me, "Breathe. Become yourself." And I did. From that moment
on I have been transformed. The world has opened up for me. I am
becoming the me that God intended. The smoke screen is gone. The
world is more clear, I am a part of life. It was truly a miracle.

*Today, I will remember that it is a miracle when I do not smoke, a
gift from God, and I will accept this gift of breath and life.*

If there is light in the soul, there will be beauty in the person. If there is beauty in the person, there will be harmony in the house. If there is harmony in the house, there will be order in the nation. If there is order in the nation, there will be peace in the world.

—CHINESE PROVERB

Could it be that if I get my act together it will reflect outward to affect the rest of the world? I look at this proverb to mean the world of my community and everyone I come into contact with. I cannot say how many times something someone has said in a meeting has deeply affected me and given me an opportunity to see a situation in a new way, thereby releasing my fear or anxiety or hurt. And who knows, perhaps that one person who has touched me will touch others through me because of what I have learned. The possibilities are endless. What we have is of value to someone else. We must share it.

Today, I will release my shyness and insecurity so I can share my "experience, strength and hope" with others.

Celebrate all of it.
—UNKNOWN

I am not sure if I wrote this quote or read it somewhere. It is something I came up with two years ago, along with my boyfriend at the time. He was in recovery in another Twelve Step Program, and we went through some big changes, which came with some big misunderstandings and difficulties (these almost always go together).

As a tool for handling anger, disappointment, frustration and fear we would start our discussion of the subject with, "Well, we agreed to celebrate all of it, so...."

I am writing to say it helps me remain grateful for the chance to be here, feeling good, bad, happy, sad, etc.

Today, I will seek opportunities to conquer one of my fears. I believe I can do this with the help available to me.

If you are going to doubt something,
doubt your limits.

—DON WARD

Now that I am off nicotine, I have the opportunity to look at my stuff more carefully. It is amazing how I limit myself, and how limitless the possibilities are. If I believe I am worthless, it will take a lot on the part of someone else to convince me otherwise. But if every day I expand my belief in the possibilities available to me, imagine what wonderful things could happen. Perhaps I should stop doubting myself and begin doubting my limits.

Today, I will look for ways I am limiting myself, gently release the limitation, and envision a more limitless life.

> If the only prayer you ever say is "thanks,"
> it is enough.
>
> —MEISTER ECKHART

Since I started coming to Nicotine Anonymous, I seem to be saying "thanks" all the time. Thank you. Thanks for another day nicotine-free. Thanks for being at the meeting tonight, everyone, and helping me; it has been a rough day. Thanks for the Serenity Prayer, which I repeat over and over throughout my days. Thanks for the encouraging books and pamphlets, for your funny story, for that helpful reminder.

There are a lot of ways to pray: sitting cross-legged on my aging sit-bones; kneeling on my creaking knees; sitting quietly, listening; walking in nature; joining in community in church; singing in fellowship; inviting peace within so it spreads all around this small earth.

John F. Kennedy said, "Peace is a daily, a weekly, a monthly process." For someone in recovery, it is indeed a daily process inviting peace inside.

Today, I will pray to say thanks
and to invite peace inside.

Compassion is forgiving others;
wisdom is forgiving yourself.
—BUDDHA

When I started working on Steps Four through Ten, I had a really hard time listing my own strengths and assets. It was easy to list all my defects. It was like a litany, "I have this defect, and this one, and this one." But it was so much harder to say, "I am proud of the fact that I …," or "I am really good at …" When it came time to make amends, it was so difficult to forgive myself (and sometimes still is). I like to remember that forgiving myself is an integral part of "working the Steps." Yes I make mistakes, but I am starting again and must let go of my self-hatred in order to grow.

Today, Higher Power, thank you for my strengths and assets. I will use them.

I had another smoking dream last night.

—NICOTINE ANONYMOUS MEMBER

I have over five years off nicotine and I still have smoking dreams. What is that about? I figure it is because I will always be an addict, no matter how many years I am off nicotine. There is a part of me that still wants to turn to nicotine when I get hurt, or angry, or afraid, even if I am not consciously aware of it. I have started to see those dreams as reminders that I will never not be a nicotine addict. But through the grace of my Higher Power, day by day, I also remember that I do not need nicotine today.

Today, my dream is to be "happy, joyous, and free," and with the help of my Higher Power my dream becomes reality.

I forgive myself for judging my feelings.
I forgive myself for becoming upset and moving
out of my center.
I forgive myself for the mistakes I have made, the
mistakes I am making and the mistakes I will make.
I forgive myself for judging myself unworthy.
I am a radiant being filled with light and love.

—UNKNOWN

This affirmation is filled with so much: forgiveness being the main lesson, forgiveness of ourselves. How many times do I do these things: getting upset with myself, trashing myself for my human mistakes, and most of all constantly judging myself? How hard it is to see that I am perfect right now in my imperfections? I am a being who is meant to grow; that is what makes me human and it is one of the great joys of life. I can learn, grow, apologize and change my life into something I am proud of. The Steps help with this of course, but also the act of remembering that I am a radiant being filled with light and love.

*Today, I will remember that I am human and that
as I love others, so too will I be loved.*

Fear and anxiety can be teaching tools.
—NICOTINE ANONYMOUS MEMBER

I read a book once that talked about master teachers. These are people, things, and events that come into our lives to help us grow. Sometimes it is painful. It is kind of wonderful to think that all those things that cause me pain and anguish are really in my life to help me grow. I can look at my fear and ask myself why I am afraid. Perhaps if I can answer that question I will have released myself from yet another defect. Suddenly all those things that I have avoided in my life can actually help me. It is so liberating.

Today, if something goes wrong I'm going to look at it as a lesson to learn.

A saint is a sinner who keeps on trying.
—BERNARD CARGES

Remembering my imperfections are normal, human and forgivable is important. No saint was ever perfect. We all have saintly qualities and our connection to the community of Nicotine Anonymous is part of this. As I work the Steps, sponsor others, do service, share at meetings, I am continuing to try to improve my life and give back to others. It is a worthwhile endeavor. I cannot lose.

Today, I will remember that as I try my
hardest to improve my life and others' lives
that I am being the best that I can be.

And as we let our light shine, we unconsciously
give other people permission to do the same. As
we are liberated from our own fear, our presence
automatically liberates others.

—MARIANNE WILLIAMSON

I love going to meetings and hearing others tell of how they are growing, or have overcome a fear. As I see them grow and challenge old ideas so then do I have more courage to challenge my own fears and beliefs. This Program provides so much for each member through the presence of all the other members. We are all teaching each other and showing by our own examples that we can live without nicotine and can replace it with self-love, discovery, sharing, and courage. What a gift.

*Today, I will let my light shine so that
others can see new possibilities.*

The feeling will pass,
whether we use nicotine or not.
—NICOTINE ANONYMOUS: THE BOOK

What I am trying to grab hold of is to notice, feel, and experience the feeling, then let it go, not attach to it. This relates to anger, yelling at people, acting out, doing destructive actions to myself and/or others, avoidance, resistance, laziness, fear, jealousy, crazy behavior in general, and to just notice anything that is not clear or love.

Today, I will notice the thought or feeling, and act on it if it is correct, or if not let it go. It will pass whether I use nicotine or not.

> The real voyage of discovery consists not in
> seeking new landscapes, but in having new eyes.
>
> —MARCEL PROUST

It took me a long time and several relapses before I realized that I could never be secure in my freedom until I realized what I was up against. This was a spiritual battle I was fighting.

Relapse knocked me back into the trenches and kept my head down in the dirt. Only in retrospect can I see how this fight showed itself in a battle with my own values. I said I valued my health and my life, yet I continued to use tobacco. I said I valued my Nicotine Anonymous group but during a relapse, I let too much pride and shame keep me away.

I knew there was a Higher Power willing to help me carry this burden, but instead of reaching out in the darkness of my own despair, I almost succumbed to the thought that there was no hope left for me. I would die of my addiction. Where do these thoughts come from?

Only through the grace of my Higher Power did I come to the point where I could truly whisper, "help." And that has made all the difference in the world.

---

*Today, I will remember that taking a
leap of faith can give me super power.*

The great thing to learn about life is, first not to do
what you don't want to do, and second, to do
what you do want to do.

—MARGARET C. ANDERSON

I am becoming reacquainted with a long-forgotten side of myself. A part of me is now liberated from the dictatorship of nicotine addiction.

With each passing day I feel grateful to be free of something so harmful to me and to those around me. I no longer have to keep track of how many cigarettes I have or if there will be enough to last until the next day. When going out for the evening I do not have to strategically plan when I can slip away for a quick smoke, then try to conceal the evidence with too many breath mints and too much perfume.

There is such a sense of liberation now when I prepare to go anywhere. I no longer have to consider if there is enough room in my purse or pocket for my cigarettes and lighter. I do not have to worry if I will have enough to get me through the evening or if someone will inadvertently keep my lighter.

Gone are the days of panic and frustration, worrying if there is a smoking section or not. I am free from smelling like the bottom of an ashtray. I am free from the awful burning sensation in my lungs the morning after a night of heavy smoking. I am free to feel good about myself. I am free.

Today, I rejoice in my freedom.

Two little words that can make the difference:
Start Now.
—MARY C. CROWLEY

I never thought I would admit this, but when I was smoking I thought that I was in control. I told people that I smoked because I like to smoke. I did not realize that I smoked because I was addicted. I did not realize that my addiction to nicotine had consumed my entire life. There was not a place I could go without cigarettes. Back then, it was even acceptable to smoke in a hospital. Even as a patient, you could have an ashtray brought to you.

Things started to change. Smoking was not acceptable. I started getting upset with the new rules. Then I realized that the universe was preparing me for my new journey. I was no longer allowed to smoke at work. Several friends did not allow smoking in their houses. Restaurants were making non-smoking sections. Things were changing, but I was not ready to change. It took a long time for me to accept the fact that I was not smoking for enjoyment. Nicotine had the upper hand.

Now that I am smober, I realize that all these changes in the world are a real help to me. They were tiny, little stepping stones for me to use to get ready to quit, and stay quit. They were getting me ready to start taking steps to freedom. At the time, I did not know that it would be the Twelve Steps.

Today, I am grateful for giving
my consent to a better life.

> The elevator of success is out of order today. You're going to
> have to take the stairway, one step at a time.
> —DR. WAYNE W. DYER

Every time I thought of quitting, I would look for the newest
product on the market. I was looking for an easy way to quit. I
did not want to feel the pain or discomfort of withdrawal.
Needless to say, there are always new products, for people just like me. I
probably spent as much money on items to quit smoking as I did on
tobacco.

The best part of my quitting was finding the Twelve Steps. Yes, I
have had to climb them "one Step at a time." Yes, I have slipped back
once in a while, and had to start over again. And yes, I am still free from
nicotine. It has been twenty-two months. I rarely think of the amount of
time. I just take it "one day at a time," and I remember to express my
gratitude each and every day.

---

*Today, I will remember that anything worth
doing is best done "one Step at a time."*

> The greatness of a man's power is
> the measure of his surrender.
>
> —WILLIAM BOOTH

I give up. I just give up. These magic words released the bondage nicotine had over me. Surrender is the word for what happened when I truly accepted the pathological description of addiction. Enormous mental, physical and emotional energy went into the struggle. I just let it go.

When I surrender, I let go of all the chaos. I focus on new strategies. I redirect my mental energy towards help, help from outside of myself.

Perhaps you, like me, know people who died trying to take charge and control their addiction, instead of accepting the reality that nicotine was in charge.

The noun addict is not such a bad word anymore. It is what I am. But being an addict does not mean feeding my addiction.

Today, I will remember strength comes through acceptance and surrender.

Today, I will try not to play small but love myself enough to step into my brilliance.

> Let us train our minds to desire
> what the situation demands.
>
> —LUCIUS ANNAEUS SENECA

There was a time, when I was in the process of giving up my nicotine substitute after successfully quitting smoking. It was a difficult time for me. I was afraid to be without nicotine, just like I had been afraid to be without cigarettes.

It was suggested that I write a personal Third Step prayer in my own words. I sat down, and wrote a very meaningful prayer. I decided to type the prayer on small cards that I could keep in key places, to remember to say the prayer throughout the day.

I typed a "t" where a "w" should have been. It still was a word, so the spell check did not catch the error. To my horror, in the middle of the prayer, the line that was to be, "I am now willing to ask for help," read instead, "I am not willing to ask for help." What a shock. Was that my subconscious teaching me something? It made me ask myself if I was really willing.

I decided to retype the cards to read, "I am (now OR not) willing to ask for help." I need to make a choice each time I say my beautiful, personal Third Step Prayer.

*Today, I will ask my Higher Power to
help me to make the correct choice.*

Our soul develops as does the pearl—
through irritation.
—ROKELLE LERNER

Looking back at my life I realize if I had not gone through some of the worst times on my life's journey, I would not have found out some wonderful things, like just how much strength I really do have. I discovered perseverance, patience and maturity seldom arrive until I was faced with some failure or adversity. Eventually through trial and error and not giving up, persistence pays off.

I would not have elected to go through a divorce, lose a job, or get a diagnosis that scares the heck out of me. Yet, sometimes the very thing I fear the most is actually the ticket to an entirely new world opening up where before there was none.

Recovery brought me to a new road that can take me to places I had never imagined. I discovered not having to wait for a seat in a restaurant, and not canceling a trip out west to visit Aunt Mary just because it would mean sitting in an airplane for four hours.

Yet the most important gift of recovery is the simple but unbelievable good feeling from knowing I have conquered something that once had me tied up in knots. The knots are unraveling, and I will keep working on them.

*Today, I welcome challenges knowing what
does not break me, makes me stronger.*

Everything depends on what the people
are capable of wanting.

—ENRICO MALATESTA

I used to resist change out of fear of the unknown, wishing to stay with the status quo because it was familiar. Now, because of the Twelve Steps of Nicotine Anonymous, I have learned to look forward to change, to welcome it and react to it with a positive frame of mind instead of self-pity based fear. I have also learned to accept unexpected change with joy and gratitude instead of irritability and discontent.

My life was unmanageable. I was a slave to nicotine. When I finally made the decision to "turn my will and my life over to God as I understood Him," and asked God to lift my obsession to nicotine, God did. Now I do not run to nicotine when I am fearful, angry or sad. Instead I try to face my feelings and then let them go. I do not do this perfectly; I am only human. I grow when I can remember to react with unconditional love, acceptance, and gratitude. The change benefits me in ways I could not have seen if I had resisted. I have learned that God often sends me a hidden pearl in disguise.

*Today, with every person or circumstance
that comes my way, I have a choice. My
choice is simply how I respond.*

A winner makes commitments—
a loser makes promises.
—CREATIVE PERFORMANCE INSTITUTE

How many times had I said, "I promise to quit smoking when (fill in the blanks) is over." I would go through the motions of quitting, but always in the back of my mind leave the door open, just wide enough to where my addiction would come bursting through unannounced and lay me out flat.

Finally I made the decision; I closed the door. I promised to just close it for today. I only need to commit to today. Let tomorrow take care of itself.

Whenever I hear myself say, "I can't," I check to see if I am really saying, "I won't." There's a world of difference between can't and won't.

Today, I will check to see what I
really mean if I say, "I can't."

For everything there is a season, and a time
for every matter under heaven....
—THE BIBLE

This is one of the quotations from the bible that always moved me. Now is the time for me to quit nicotine. I used nicotine for thirty-one years and for twenty-eight of those years I told myself I was going to quit. I had my last nicotine fix September 30, 2003.

About two months ago I was given a list of places to call for help. On the list was the Nicotine Anonymous information number. I called the number for directions to the meeting not knowing if I should attend or not. I know I need someone or more than one person to report to. I want to say, "I have been nicotine-free since September 30, 2003." The Nicotine Anonymous meetings give me that opportunity.

*Today, I will reach out and
accept the support I need.*

OCTOBER 1

We get too soon old and too late smart.

—FRANK KELLY FREAS

If only I knew then what I know now, how different my life would have been. The unfolding of my life sometimes involves regrets. If only I never started using tobacco. If only I never started again after my pregnancy. If only I had not relapsed after my mother's funeral. The regrets can keep me awake at night.

Unfortunately, sometimes I can only evaluate decisions in retrospect.

From the start I knew that beginning recovery was a decision I would never regret. No matter how difficult or easy it turned out to be, in the bottom of my heart, I knew that this decision was close to being one of the best, most intelligent decisions I have ever made.

I think of all the times I relapsed. I think of others who never made the decision, whose funerals I have attended.

Today, I will embrace decisions I know
are right and accept those that turn out
differently than I expected.

We ask ourselves, "Who am I to be brilliant,
gorgeous, talented, fabulous?" Actually, who are
you not to be? You are a child of God. Your
playing small does not serve the world.
—MARIANNE WILLIAMSON

It was hard for me to realize that I was a skilled and capable individual. I had such low self-esteem, and always found the comfort of nicotine to help in situations when I felt low.

Now that I am no longer using nicotine and have been a member of Nicotine Anonymous over five years, I am finding that I have leadership qualities. People in meetings appreciate me and my ideas; I have taken on service and feel I have something to contribute. It feels good. I am still shy about my skills and attributes, but I am working on it.

*Today, I will not play small but love myself
enough to step into my brilliance.*

We must be able to make use
of our special gifts.
—RICHARD LEIDER

I am amazed at all the talented, creative people I have met through this Program. It seems like too many of them died before their talents matured and blossomed.

I believe we all start these lives of ours prepackaged with certain talents and gifts that sometimes we only discover way down the years. My addiction caused me to feel I had few talents and dreams.

I used to think, "Oh, I get it, you don't have any talents; your life has no purpose; don't even try to stop smoking, you'll never make it."

Now that I am free of my addiction, I am confident I can do anything. Shall I learn how to play the guitar? Perhaps I will take up bike riding, or play tennis or paint a picture? I have a pile of creative seeds waiting to be opened. I even see how I can make a positive difference inspiring others.

*Today, I will honor my dreams
and ask, "why not?"*

One is never afraid of the unknown; one is afraid
of the known coming to an end.

—JIDDU KRISHNAMURTI

How often I have gotten caught in fear of an old association with nicotine. Many times I felt frozen by fear, but I did not have to be. For years I gave in to the fear of being without cigarettes, until I realized I smoked two-thirds of my life away.

I do not have to be stuck in fear. After all if that were the case I, like many other members of Nicotine Anonymous, would never have gotten through my first day free of nicotine, since I never imagined I could function without it. The same holds true for the first Thanksgiving, first New Year's, first birthday, and first visits back to places and events where I once smoked.

Now without nicotine to bury emotions, not to mention me, I am learning how to feel fear and accept it. All of the old memories are starting to be replaced with new ones, memories filled with deep breaths and freedom, free of nicotine and all of the ills that went with it. Thank God.

*Today, I reflect on the willingness I felt to let
go of the fear life without nicotine. I will let
willingness work in other areas of my life.*

> For peace of mind, resign as general
> manager of the universe.
>
> —LARRY EISENBERG

How many times had I tried to control my tobacco use and failed, five, ten, fifteen, a thousand times?

Controlling an addiction is like trying to lasso a cloud and wondering why it does not rain. I also tried to control people, places or situations. That did not work either.

I used to say, "Quitting smoking is no problem. I could quit anytime." I just needed to get everything exactly where I thought it needed to be before I quit. My kids would have to stop bugging me. My job would have to be less stressful. Blah ... blah ... blah ... blah ... blah.

How many years ago was that? I found life just does not work that way. Gaining freedom was just the opposite. I let go of control, surrendered my, "I can quit anytime I want to but now is not the right time," attitude and humbly started to listen, really listen to what others who had been there said and did.

I actually learned that when I was struggling, I could pick up the phone and call someone. Or I could email them an alert that I was having a hard time. I stopped trying to fix everything myself. I let go of control for a moment and said, "It's okay that I don't have all the answers." What a relief that was.

Today, I will look for acceptance,
courage and wisdom.

I have lost my smile, But don't worry.
The dandelion has it.
—CITED BY THICH NHAT HANH

When I am feeling stuck by the cravings or temptations or my resentment or my problems, I just need a small moment of gratitude to break the spell and revitalize hope; it releases me to remember how to do what it takes to get back on program. Sitting in the sunshine, taking a walk, spending time with a special loved one, or just sitting down to write ten things I can choose to be happy about can turn my whole day around.

Today, I can remember
gratitude fosters hope.

God is a set of powers surrounding me
and always available to me.
—NICOTINE ANONYMOUS MEMBER

God loves me. I know this because He gave me the strength to stop smoking cigarettes, "one day at a time." He is always there for me no matter what. I ask Him to help me with anything and everything in my life. And when I ask (I have to ask) I always get help. I always get love and support. I always get to grow from what I get.

Today, I will remember to "let go and let God."

You give your time to doubt and fear when no value
comes of that. Better to give time to the journey inward,
to that voice that needs you to sound its truth.

—JAN PHILLIPS

I am learning to be open to the possibilities my Higher Power has in store for me. Sometimes when fear comes, it is because I need to pay attention to something; maybe to stop and see what I need to do next, like change my course.

I have noticed when second hand smoke bothers me it is usually because there is something I need to address, like a physical need, or an emotion I am suppressing. In such a case fear can be a helpful emotion. However, like all things in life, it has a flip side. It can also be a hindrance to me.

Sometimes fear is just a feeling that is best dealt with by accepting it. A Twelve Step slogan labels it, "False Evidence Appearing Real." I cannot help but think of all of the times I have not acted because I was immobilized by fear. I imagine my life could have been different if I had just accepted certain fears and gone on. The good news is that it is never too late to start over, and I can learn now.

Today, when facing anything scary, I
will breathe and ask God for help.

The love of our neighbor in all its fullness
simply means being able to say to him,
"What are you going through?"
—SIMONE WEIL

I went to my first Nicotine Anonymous meeting for one reason. I wanted to quit using a deadly drug that had me under its spell. I never realized that the journey of "working the Steps" would land me at Step Twelve and bring more joy by sharing my "experience, strength and hope" with others.

Little by little the gratitude for my new freedom evolved into "carrying the message." I do that by making coffee, setting up the room, returning a phone call, providing a brief hug. These actions help to keep the meeting going for those new to the Program.

Who would have thought that the sharing of my gifts would be so easy? And where would I be if I had stopped going to meetings and the Nicotine Anonymous group was no more? I developed compassion for those still suffering and continue to allow my life to be an example and support for others.

Today, I will share my joy
through little acts of compassion.

In the face of uncertainty, there is
nothing wrong with hope.
—DR. BERNIE SIEGEL

When I first walked into a Nicotine Anonymous meeting, I was amazed at what I saw. In a large room were nicotine addicts, who like me were trying to stay quit. We gathered in strength and unity to surrender to a Power greater than ourselves. We shared our experiences and successes over the days, months, and years. Without a question, this Program was the key to unleash me from my self-torture.

My task was not as insurmountable as I once had thought. I had to go beyond wishing. I could do what others have done before me. I now had to grasp the belief and convictions of what I a saw with my own eyes. I learned prayers that saved me time and time again. I learned to develop a quiet mind and a loving heart. I learned to surrender to a Power greater than myself, and most importantly to stay in conscious contact.

Today, I realize the job that needs to be done has a definite timeline. Stretching my imagination is no substitute for hard work and application.

A primary reason people don't do new things is because
they want to do them perfectly, first time.

—PETER MCWILLIAMS

When I realized I was powerless over my quitting smoking, and that I was totally and miserably addicted, I also realized that I did not know how to stop. I also did not really know if I could.

I did all kinds of research to get ready in case I would or could quit one day. I looked into patches, herbal remedies, laser therapy, rehabs, etc. I thought for me to quit I needed my hands to be tied up and my mouth taped shut and my body confined somewhere.

Coincidences, although I really believe there are none, were placed in my path with information about a smoking cessation class. At this point I realized I am responsible to try something. It does not have to and probably will not work, but I need to try. I went. I did not believe what was said there. I listened. And I tried. One hour turned into two and then little by slowly twenty-four. Gee, if I could do twenty-four, I will try another twenty-four. I took direction and went to Nicotine Anonymous when the class was over, and by some miracle I am still not smoking today. I need to do a little footwork and let the God of my understanding do the rest.

*Today, I will stop to see what footwork
I need to do and let God do the rest.*

> To man belong the plans of the heart, but from the
> Lord comes the reply of the tongue.
>
> —THE BIBLE

I did not know what this meant. A footnote says it means that the final outcome of the plans we make is in God's hands. If so, why make plans? In doing God's will, there must be partnership between my efforts and God's control. God wants me to seek the advice of others, and to plan. Nevertheless, the results are up to God. Planning helps me act God's way.

This giving up control in all things is difficult but doable. I may take control back when things are not going as I like or expect. I may make little effort and then wonder why I do not succeed.

When I tried to stop smoking, I made several attempts, a day or a week then I would go back to smoking. Finally, I realized I was trying to do it alone, "white-knuckling it" instead of "turning it over" to God. I even felt others could do it but I could not. I had to take "one day at a time" or one minute at a time. I did the footwork: calling others when cravings were strong; diverting my attention by changing my activity; reading the "Serenity Prayer for Smokers" over and over; praying for willingness.

Today, I will trust my Higher Power
and release the outcome.

OCTOBER 13

I believe that we learn by practice. Whether it
means to learn to dance by practicing dancing or
to learn to live by practicing living, the principles
are the same.

—MARTHA GRAHAM

Turning over my will and life to the care of God means to me
that I must do things, often different things, to nurture and
grow in sobriety. Nicotine says I need more of it; I say I need
more of God.

Recovery means calling someone who will listen to and encourage
me. I have learned to believe in those who have succeeded, to do service
work, to surrender the outcome of my day. My Higher Power always has
wonderful gifts that come when I am ready, taking action, and watching.

*Today, I will be as diligent in my recovery as
I was in maintaining my addiction.*

In any instant the sacred may wipe you with its
finger. In any instant you may avail yourself of the
power to love your enemies; to accept failure,
slander, or the grief of loss, or to endure torture.

—ANNIE DILLARD

"Where does it hurt?" my sponsor once asked me. "What do you mean?" I asked. "Well you said quitting smoking hurts so bad, and I am asking where it hurts."
After I got over the anger I thought it is very difficult to pinpoint where or how it hurts exactly. I need the Sacred, the Higher Power, God, to help me endure my pain and sense of torture to truly live "happy, joyous and free." Very often when I do not like the way I feel, I do not know (or care) where it hurts.

I feel I have been touched by the Sacred through the experiences of the Twelve Steps and our Fellowship and I am so grateful.

Thank you God, for this gift of life shared with you, even though at times it hurts so bad. I know this experience of a sober life is a true gift of God.

*Today, I thank God for the ability to live life
fully without resorting to nicotine.*

After all the failures, all the false starts, all the best
intentions, there was little hope.

—NICOTINE ANONYMOUS: THE BOOK

"One day at a time" is all I need to deal with. I had so many failures at quitting tobacco over so many years, when I got to Nicotine Anonymous I had little faith I could quit. But it has been working for over seven years. I am now free of nicotine, and I am so grateful.

I turn the problem of addiction over to God every morning when I wake up, and say, "Thank You God for another day of freedom" every night right before I go to bed, "one day at a time."

In the beginning I needed to accept the pain of withdrawal and cravings that were so strong at times. I relied on knowing I had turned the problem over to God and did not want to take it back.

Today, I will focus just on
the moment and be grateful.

Greatness lies not in being strong but in
the right use of strength.

—HENRY WARD BEECHER

I have a small smooth stone I painted and wrote the same message on both sides. The message is "turn it over."

So when I have a problem and do not know the solution I try to remember to "turn it over" to God. God will help me find the answer to the problem if I am patient and "turn it over."

Instead of using tobacco when I need to deal with a problem or wasting hours of worrying time or sleepless nights, I actually deal with the problem. Sometimes dealing with the problem means admitting I do not know what to do and knowing that God will help me. Instead of medicating myself with tobacco and trying to ignore problems that get worse over time, I turn to God for help.

I pray and remember that God is always here to help, if I remember to "turn it over" and take the necessary action when the time is right.

Today, I will consciously release any
difficulty and "turn it over" to God.

Dance first. Think later.
It's the natural order.
—SAMUEL BECKETT

I found the first three Steps of the Nicotine Anonymous Program were the beginnings of my recovery. There are two popular ways of describing the purpose of the first three Steps.
The first is: "I can't. He can. Let Him."
The second is: "Step One describes the problem; Step Two describes the solution and Step Three describes the way to get out of the problem and into the solution."
Some may say they turn things over on a daily basis with Step Three. This implies action. For me, Step Three is not an action Step; Step Three involves only a decision. With a decision there usually follows some kind of action. Over and over again, I remind myself not to complicate these simple ideas. These are simple Steps for my complicated life. Confusion, rationalization and excuse making are my greatest enemies. Honesty, open-mindedness and willingness are my greatest friends.
I acknowledge the first three Steps as a doorway to recovery from nicotine. I will not complicate or explain them away. I will enter the doorway, take them to the best of my ability, and move through the doorway. True recovery continues in Steps Four through Twelve, on the other side of the doorway.

Today, I will focus on the simple truths.

It is not enough to say I am earning enough to live and support my family; I do my work well; I am a good father; I am a good husband.... Seek always to do some good, somewhere.... For remember, you don't live in a world all your own. Your brothers are here too.

—ALBERT SCHWEITZER

When I read this quote I realized this is about Step Twelve. We have come to this marvelous Program, we have been altered, healed, helped, and supported by the people we have met who share their lives with us. It is such an amazing gift to be able to give something back, to make that extra effort to help someone else. It not only keeps us free from our addiction, it improves the world. Each small act we make outside of ourselves toward someone else in need reflects outward to the world around us, like ripples in a pond.

Today, Higher Power, please help me to remember that every action I take today has consequences tomorrow.

I notice well that one stray step from the habitual path
leads irresistibly into a new direction. Life moves
forward, it never reverses its course.

—FRANZ GRILLPARZER

My husband mentioned a friend of ours we had not heard from
in many years. I remembered an incident that happened the
last time we saw him, probably twenty-five years ago: I had
been acting in a self-deprecating manner, saying I was not good enough
or something to that effect. Our friend said to me, "You know, that just
doesn't work with me any more, because I know you are capable of more
than you think, and you know it, too."

I was dumbfounded. He had found me out. He had named my game.
I had been rooted out of the darkness and placed in the light. It was at
that moment that I began to change, and began learning to appreciate
myself and my capabilities. I realize that person who I have not seen in
many years, and to whom I have not spoken, has done me a great service
by speaking the truth, and for that I am very grateful. It occurs to me
that we have no idea how our words and actions will affect others.

*Today, Higher Power, help me to be aware of
the things I say to others and to be sure I am
always loving and honest.*

One who fears failure limits his activities.
Failure is only the opportunity to more
intelligently begin again.

—HENRY FORD

It was hard for me to think of not having cigarettes forever. In fact, it still is.

After a few months of meetings, still smoking, I tried to be free for a day. I think I made a deal with my Higher Power. I am grateful that the unsuccessful attempt the previous night to "never smoke again" did not ruin my faith in this Power greater than myself. I was willing to not smoke for just a day, just until sundown. I kept busy. The last few minutes seemed like hours, but I did it and I did not die without my "crutch."

True, I was not one hundred percent ready to be free yet, but this was some kind of progress. I miraculously saw this as a success, not my usual way of thinking. I shared it at the next meeting, and we all got a good laugh out of it. It left me open and willing for the opportunity a few days later to wonder, "What if I don't buy that next pack?"

Another miracle came through due to willingness. I could not see past that moment. If I had, I would have anticipated the fear of being without my beloved cigarettes and just bought that next pack.

---

*Today, when fears of future moments wash
over me, I will breathe and ask my Higher
Power for help to stay in this moment.*

When you're away, I'm restless, lonely, wretched,
bored, dejected; only here's the rub my darling
dear, I feel the same when you are near.
—SAMUEL HOFFENSTEIN

How I missed my little tobacco friends when I first stop putting them into my mouth. I felt deprived and abandoned. These are very common experiences when we first let go. Even when I was still using, just the anticipation of being deprived was enough to keep me from attempting to quit.

After some time in recovery I accepted that even before I quit I had felt restless, lonely, wretched, bored, dejected. Once I used the drug to numb these feelings and may even have been unaware of what I was feeling. With recovery I discovered a full range of feelings. Some are be new. Some are just more intense. Often they visit unexpectedly.

The support and the common bond I developed in our Fellowship help me come to know, that I have gained and not lost friends. The Twelve Steps help guide me so I can handle and enjoy this fuller life.

*Today, I am grateful to know what I am
feeling so that I can respond and attend to it
in a sane and healthy manner.*

For the most part, we weren't taught to set our
own goals and to achieve them.

—PETER MCWILLIAMS

I had no intention of quitting. My boss knew I smoked and he was a
real health nut. You know the type. He suggested I attend a smoking
cessation program. He would pay me my regular wage plus he bet
that I could not quit through the end of the school year. Ten dollars was
on the line; I was a starving student and would do anything for ten
bucks.

I had intended to just show up, possibly do what they suggested and
definitely quit for the next few months. Well, my Higher Power took
over. Someone I knew from another Fellowship was there and gave me
some really helpful tips on what to do instead of smoking. I ended up
quitting two days before my February quit date.

For the next few months I would cross off each day without a
cigarette. I chewed gum a lot, carried pretzels and sucked on candy. I
truly just took it "one day at a time," sometimes one minute at a time.
My boyfriend still smoked, but that did not seem to bother me. I
relapsed in June. It was such a stressful time: finals week; I broke up with
my boyfriend. I lit up a stale butt of my boyfriend's. Within two days, I
was smoking even more than before.

I celebrated my sobriety date from alcohol by quitting nicotine.

Today, I am grateful for friends who
encourage me to be the best possible me.

There are two things to aim at in life: first to get
what you want and after that, to enjoy it.
—LOGAN PEARSAL SMITH

When I see another person hurting him or herself by using nicotine, I usually go through a range of emotions, desire is one and I need to admit it.

Meetings come in handy. I once shared at a meeting that I liked the smell. Another member reminded me that when we choose our words wisely, we affect our thinking positively. So my new terminology is to admit that yes I may feel passing desire to use the stuff, but I do not say I like it.

I have also felt jealousy and anger about others using nicotine near me. After talking with my sponsor about it at length, I have sometimes been willing to realize that this person is actually me, and I can have compassion for them. I can remember that they may look glamorous or suave, but their insides are not. Insides have become a lot more important to me these days, and remembering that mine are healing from the deadly damage I did is very helpful. For the twenty years as an active nicotine addict, I did not know I could get free of it, or that I was worth it.

*Today, when I feel uncomfortable I will draw
serenity from my gratitude for the love and support
I receive from my groups and my Higher Power.*

Love your neighbor as yourself.
—THE BIBLE

Every time I used nicotine, I partook in such negativity. I was not only killing myself, but hating myself too. I became very good at feeling inferior as well as judging myself as stupid and sneaky. The inferiority I felt as a child made trying smoking so easy. Even though I thought it was disgusting at first, it was my sense of inferiority that made it so easy for me to buy my first pack and practice smoking by myself months later.

The inferiority was often replaced with a false sense of superiority which, ironically, I also felt about my smoking. When I finally entered Nicotine Anonymous and therefore recovery, I was able to entertain the idea that maybe I was worth it.

Now when I see someone still using nicotine, even though it may bother me, I am closer to remembering that I was once in his or her shoes. I look to my Higher Power and the power of my sponsor and Nicotine Anonymous friends to help me remember that we are all equal.

Today I will remember that my negative thinking is not written in stone.

Success is not final, failure is not fatal; it is the
courage to continue that counts.

—WINSTON CHURCHILL

I got very sick from cigarettes. I started smoking in a board and care home. Everyone smoked. There was nothing else to do. We were all over-medicated. I was about forty years old, and mostly I needed housing.

I smoked cigarettes made from loose tobacco. When I ran out of money I would panic. I would grub butts, buy single cigarettes with change, or beg smokes. After eight years I got sick from smoking. I got a very bad cold that would not go away. All winter I coughed and coughed and wet my pants. I smelled of urine and nicotine and ended up in adult diapers.

I got desperate and went to Nicotine Anonymous. I listened and bought the books, but felt I could not quit. After three or four months of meetings I was able to quit.

Then I quit going to meetings but stayed smoke-free for about two years. The cravings were driving me crazy so I smoked. I went back to Nicotine Anonymous. This time my recovery was slower. Now I lead a day-at-a-time meeting. I love recovery.

Today, I realize I cannot keep my recovery
unless I give it away.

You don't have to believe
everything you think.
—BUMPER STICKER

Freedom from nicotine is beyond anything my imagination could ever dream up. And believe me, it can dream up quite a lot. My Higher Power's imagination is so much bigger than mine. In any given challenge, I am learning to open to possibilities, just like I did when I became willing to not buy that next pack of nicotine delivery.

I am also learning that just because I dream something, it does not have to come true. In the early days of my freedom from nicotine, I was more easily haunted in the morning by dreams in which I picked up nicotine. I dreamed I picked up nicotine on my twelfth day of recovery. I talked about it in my meeting and found others who shared that they also had similar dreams from time to time.

I have since had many dreams like this. Happily in one I was actually able to decline an offer to use. Either way, I am learning to accept that these dreams, although unconscious, are cravings for nicotine. I now know the disease will go to any length. I am ready to match it by strengthening my recovery by making a phone call, going to a meeting, reading literature or doing service.

*Today, I will be gentle with myself, and
simply release any dreams or fantasies that
get in the way of my recovery.*

When one of his Hasids complained of God's
hiddenness, Rabbi Pinhas said "It ceases to be a hiding,
if you know it is hiding." But it does not cease to hide,
not ever, not under any circumstance, for anyone.

—ANNIE DILLARD

Since joining our Fellowship I seek to know God as I understand
God, unafraid, I hope, of what results I will or will not get. God is a
beautiful divine mystery to me and I am so grateful for the spiritual
experiences I have felt that are talked about in Step Twelve.

My worst problem, my powerlessness over my fatal addictions,
became my saving grace to bring me into contact with God. Not the God
I thought I knew through childhood experiences with religion and
people, but through a genuine adult contact with God on a deeply
personal level. The flimsy reed talked about in Alcoholics Anonymous
truly becomes the powerful loving hand of God when I let it. Hidden
yes, but hidden inside me in much the same way as I am often hidden to
myself.

*Today, I thank God for our Twelve Steps and for
being a loving and powerful presence in my life.*

It's not that I'm so smart; it's just
that I stay with problems longer.

—ALBERT EINSTEIN

G ood morning, God. Please help me live this brand new day free of tobacco and other drugs, one moment at a time. Help me "stay in the present," in Your will. My will brought me so much pain and so many bad choices, like lighting up and smoking so many times for so many years. I look to You God through our Twelve Steps to be "happy, joyous and free" of addiction. I know I can only stay free of tobacco today, not yesterday or tomorrow.

I can start today over any time I get off track and into my addictive thinking, resentments, selfishness, dishonesty or fears. I just visualize my Higher Power helping me press a big restart button.

As a now deceased friend once said anytime I asked, " How are you doing?"

"Any day above ground is a good day."

I pray your days are good ones. May you appreciate all you have, all your self so freely given.

Today, I will remember that
all I have is today.

I've been absolutely terrified every moment of my
life and I've never let it keep me from doing a
single thing I wanted to do.

—GEORGIA O'KEEFE

It is not the caboose that kills you. After that first cigarette or chew I had one thought, more tobacco. For years, I thought, "I will just smoke today. I will quit tomorrow (or next year, or next birthday)." In that way I smoked "one day at a time."

Now I know it is that giving in to one puff or one chew that keeps me an addict. I learned to live free of tobacco and other addictions "one day at a time." I will deal with tomorrow when it arrives.

I am learning that I can turn my addiction and my problems over to my Higher Power. My Higher Power helps me live free of what I cannot deal with myself, "one day at a time."

I do not want to ever again go through the pain of active addiction and being faced with quitting. So I remember that it is the first puff or chew that gets me.

Today, I will remember to focus on
the engine not the caboose.

The day a child realizes that all adults are
imperfect he becomes an adolescent; the day he
forgives them, he becomes an adult; the day he
forgives himself, he becomes wise.

—AIDEN NOWLAN

My family had a small farm. After the harvest, equipment was
stored temporarily in our hay barn, most of it belonged to
neighbors; we shared to save money. We were not finished
bailing hay but the barn was about a fourth full. We were counting on the
income from the sale of the excess.

My sister and I were playing in the barn when our father walked in. I
was nine or ten and she was almost five, but we were both already
sneaking cigarettes. We were smoking and threw our cigarettes into the
feed lot to keep from being found out.

Dad needed to run some errands so we piled into our car and left.
After we returned I stayed outside. I will never forget the moment I
glanced up and saw smoke curling out of the barn. I started yelling for
my dad. It seemed like it took just a few minutes for the barn to be
reduced to a smoldering heap of black and rust-colored twisted tin.

It was the first time I ever saw my dad break down and cry. I was
convinced our discarded cigarettes had started the fire that bankrupted
my family. It broke my heart, but it took another thirty-eight years to
find Nicotine Anonymous and the help to stop smoking.

*Today, I am free to make amends and
release any guilt from the past.*

Addiction is any thought that depletes
life while making it appear better.
—CLARISSE ESTES

Just one, just one cigarette would make this better. The old lie, how many times I fooled myself thinking a cigarette would change the situation. I believed the lie and picked up a cigarette only to find myself the slave of addiction one more time. Two packs later nothing had changed to improve my situation whether it was a broken relationship, a lost job, a fight with a relative or friend, the loss of our beloved dog, the sickness of a friend or any or a thousand excuses I found to justify, "just this one time to help me make it through."

Now I tell myself, "No matter what, just for today I will not smoke."

I know, although it feels like I am going to die and that my insides will rip open, I will not die and these feelings will pass.

Today, I will not smoke,
no matter what.

There is no failure except
in no longer trying.
—ELBERT HUBBARD

I know "I am a puff away from a pack a day." I had quit for three months, but gave into a craving. I took a pull from a butt and was back to smoking a pack and a half. In a month I was back to where I left off.

I knew I needed help and went to a meeting. That got me on the road to being nicotine-free. We have a meeting once a week that keeps me from using nicotine. We read the Steps and stories from *Nicotine Anonymous, The Book*.

I knew I had to stop when I got chest pains that scared me. Today, having been off nicotine for over a year, I can breathe better; I walk longer distances; food tastes better; I feel healthy, happy and full of peace. Through God's grace I am nicotine-free today. I am not hiding my feelings. I am grateful to be alive.

Today, I will pause to acknowledge my gratitude each time I am feeling stress.

Be absolutely determined
to enjoy what you do.
—GERRY SKIORSKI

I had long ago determined that there were no good reasons to continuing using nicotine. Millions of people go through life experiencing difficult circumstances, and have never felt the need to use nicotine to cope. But this realization was not in itself sufficient motivation to get me to stop. Besides, I was convinced that, for me, it was too late. I believed the damage I had done in thirty years was too severe to overcome. If I quit, I would probably die shortly thereafter from cancer or some other smoking-related disease. Why bother?

As I agonized over wanting to quit and not being able to, praying for help and willingness, two things happened. First a friend told me about Nicotine Anonymous and I began attending. Second, the thought came to me that, regardless of what happened after I quit, my quality of life would be better if I were nicotine-free. Come what may, cancer, heart disease, whatever, I would get through it better if I were not using nicotine.

Today, the quality of my life comes from my choice to welcome my Higher Power rather than nicotine.

Remember that all you need you have inside; that
wisdom you long for you already own.
—JAN PHILLIPS

I have been on a long spiritual journey, always searching for a
connection. What does the spirituality I have heard and learned
about in various services, retreats, meetings and seminars have to do
with my day-to-day life? What difference, if any, does it really make?

I smoked for forty years. I finally gave up hope of ever quitting.
Then I found Nicotine Anonymous and the Twelve Steps. I am
amazed, every day.

Something else has happened. In meetings I hear people talk about a
Higher Power; recognizing powerlessness; coming to believe that only a
Higher Power can restore our sanity; and turning over our will and our
lives to our Higher Power.

To me it is not just a question of living a better life or a more
rewarding life. It is a matter of life and death; of sanity or insanity.
Nicotine kills; using nicotine is insane.

The spirituality I am learning is saving my life and restoring me to
sanity. It is as real as the air that I breathe and the water I drink.

I came to Nicotine Anonymous to quit using nicotine. But I have
also found what I have been looking for since I was seven or eight years
old: a real, living spirituality that is not just once a week. It is every day,
every hour, every minute, every moment.

*Today, I am grateful for a spiritual path that
is real, every moment of every day.*

The only ways for an addict to quell the craving is to either: 1) admit the substance into their blood stream; or 2) not admit the substance into the blood stream. And the second way is the only permanent way.

—NICOTINE ANONYMOUS MEMBER

My name is _____ and I am a nicotine addict. Those words are so true for me. I can vividly remember despairing of ever feeling like a normal human being without nicotine. How could I ever manage to become a recovering addict? I could not imagine going without nicotine for even a few waking hours, much less days or even weeks. Whenever I stopped for more than overnight I could not see straight, my hands shook, I could not think clearly, my heart pounded, my ears rang, food did not taste right, coffee did not have any appeal, etc.

For years I tried quitting every possible way available. I quit at least once a month for the last twenty of the forty years of my active addiction.

Now after fifteen years nicotine-free, I still occasionally remember and am amazed that I feel just as good today as if I had my old level of nicotine, but I did not use today. I know first hand the only way to cope with a craving is to not use nicotine at all. I am continuously grateful that I am nicotine-free today.

Today, I will share my joy in recovery with nicotine addicts who still suffer.

The best way out
is always through.
—ROBERT FROST

I could not stop smoking after promises broken and failed attempts for decades. At age forty-five I saw a physician who diagnosed me as having emphysema. He told me unless I quit smoking I had about a year left to live.

I knew I could not stop alone. I believed in a Higher Power that had intervened in my life and saved it before, both as a child and as an adult.

I paid the doctor's receptionist and went into the restroom. On my knees there, I asked this Higher Power to remove my nicotine addiction. I then went to lunch in a nearby café where in 1983 smoking was allowed. The man next to me at the counter lit a cigarette, but I did not have to feed my own addiction. I have never smoked again.

Deeply grateful, I started Nicotine Anonymous meetings in my home city. I still attend to encourage newcomers to believe in what they cannot yet see, and to practice the Steps and principles in daily life. I attend because I am told that only if I share my recovery may I keep it and because I have learned to care.

*Today, I can and will put myself and my nicotine
addiction in God's hands and try to help someone else.*

It's always too early to quit.

—NORMAN VINCENT PEALE

A major step in my journey of recovery has been learning what it means to make a commitment. I am committed to going to meetings whether I feel like it or not, because I know being there helps me, and what I have to share may help some else.

I have expanded my commitment to recovery to include eating right and exercising, even though I do not always want to. I have made these commitments based on faith. I have faith that the Program works if I work it, and that sticking to my commitments will get easier in time.

Today, I will make one commitment
to myself, however minor, and resolve
to see it through.

The moment of victory is much too
short to live for that and nothing else.
—MARTINA NAVRATILOVA

One of the great truths I contemplate is that nothing is forever. I mean that apart from God, nothing we encounter in our lives will remain unchanged forever. Nothing even stays the same for a moment. All things are made of particles in motion. All beings are flowing streams of feeling and thought.

Realizing this is a double-edged sword. I must not become attached to the happiness I feel in times of good fortune; this too is impermanent and will surely pass away. On the other hand, I can take comfort in the fact that my problems will not last; in all likelihood, one day my ship will come in.

My life is like waves on a beach, ebbing and flowing in an ever changing cycle of ups and downs.

*Today, I accept life in
all its ebbs and flows.*

Freedom is like a birth. 'Til we are fully free,
we are slaves.
—MOHANDAS GANDHI

My life has changed in every way since I finally ended the madness of nicotine addiction. This took me many tries and the constant support of Nicotine Anonymous over years. I now have seven years of freedom.

I am free from the unending nagging of when I can smoke again, and even while smoking, wondering when I can smoke again. Will it be five minutes, an hour? I am free from sneaking out at work to buy a pack of cigarettes after I had quit the night before. I am free from having to plan every activity and all my relationships around being able to smoke.

I left my child in a pre-surgery hospital room alone when he begged me not to because I had to smoke. I let another child repeatedly leave the house when she threatened to do so because I would not put down my cigarettes just long enough to talk to her.

In the past seven years I have been able to travel, to volunteer, to work with a clear conscience, to honor my family, to be with my grandchildren, and above all to be free from the powerful enslavement of the drug nicotine.

*Today, I am grateful for the new life
I have without nicotine.*

Accentuate the positive, eliminate the
negative, latch on to the affirmative, don't
mess with Mr. In-Between.

—JOHNNY MERCER

Early in my struggle to quit using nicotine, I adopted the practice of keeping a list of every time I used, including what I was feeling at the time. I always gave up, finding keeping the list was just too much trouble.

Today, years into recovery, I realized why that method may not have succeeded. In tracking my use, I kept focusing on being deprived. My thoughts were always on the sacrifice I was making. Eventually something would happen that would be worse than the sacrifice I was willing to make.

I discovered this by using a similar approach to losing weight. I would list every thing I did to lose weight. My list included the rolls I did not eat at lunch, the cookie I skipped, the ice cream I did not have. Surely after enough incidents of doing without, I was entitled to splurge. I recognized the trap in that approach and resolved to list only positive actions. When I finally succeeding in breaking free of nicotine I had used gratitude each time I had a craving. With each craving I celebrated the fact that I no longer was enslaved to nicotine.

It was great to be reminded that each addiction or bad habit I have released has been because of a grateful heart and mind. The gifts of this Program continue to show up in my life.

*Today, I will stop and give thanks for all I have
received and all I am able to give back.*

I never knew how to worship
until I knew how to love.

—HENRY WARD BEECHER

My mother was a devout churchgoer, but despite attending church weekly, I never seemed to get what she got. I did not feel what she apparently felt, so I quit going. Throughout college I read eastern philosophy and practiced meditation and t'ai chi; those made me feel good but I still did not get it.

After joining Nicotine Anonymous I slowly understood what a spiritual connection to a Higher Power was supposed to feel like and I began to get it. The slogans, "let go and let God" and "doing the next right thing" began to give me serenity. But what was most important was the realization that I could define my Higher Power any way I wanted. It did not have to fit anyone else's definition. Today my Higher Power is helping me be serene, courageous and wise, "one day at a time."

*Today, I remember that my connection to my
Higher Power is as strong as I make it.*

Courage is fear holding on
a minute longer.
—THOMAS FULLER

I had quit many times with abstinence periods of differing lengths but
no Program. I always resumed in order to fit in, to be cool or to stifle
painful feelings or feelings of any kind. Within minutes of my
mother's death I asked a friend for a cigarette and was off and smoking
yet again after eight years of non-use.

I heard of a Nicotine Anonymous meeting in our town and went
when I finally decided I really had to stop. Even though I had never
attended a Twelve Step Program I thought I knew what they were about.
But I really did not. What I found was freedom, and not just from
nicotine. By going back week after week, through working the Program,
and accepting the cravings, I began to experience health and strength in
my body and soul. I learned I could deal with feelings in the Program by
holding on, knowing that they will surely pass as does each craving.

Step Two is there for me whenever I am ready to take it.

---

*Today, I am confident there is a Higher
Power who can restore me to sanity.*

We are rich only through what we give,
and poor only for what we refuse.

—RALPH WALDO EMERSON

Nicotine Anonymous and the Twelve Steps freed me from
nicotine and opened me to life's greater treasures. Here is one
example.

While my students were taking a quiz the other day I glanced at the
floor and noticed a glass bead. "Just let the cleaners vacuum it," I
thought. Then I wondered if perhaps it was a rhinestone from one
student's shirt, so I picked it up. It was not hers. I took a closer look and
discovered it was not a rhinestone, but a diamond. Wow, things are not
what they appear.

I asked students and staff if they had lost a stone, but could not find
the owner. By that time I really did not want to find the owner. I taped
the tiny stone to a piece of paper to save it.

Over the next few days, I told others about finding it, and became
open to the lessons. I only picked it up to be of service. A friend said
others would not have even noticed it. Another said it demonstrated that
I was open to receiving prosperity. Another was going through a very
difficult transition and saw it as an affirmation of the beauty and value
that can come from adversity.

Then I began to get caught up in the potential monetary value and
took it to a jeweler. It turned out to be a cubic zirconium.

What was my ultimate lesson? When I intended service, I discovered
value; when I turned toward greed the value disappeared.

---

*Today, I will be loving and generous
and let God take care of the rewards.*

God is pure love. Love is spirit's changeless nature.
The truth is: to forgive is human; to love is divine.
—JIM AND NANCY ROSEMERGY

I used nicotine to avoid dealing with many issues such as anger and fear. Nicotine Anonymous showed me how to deal with "life on life's terms." When I feel angry I know to look at myself rather than the other person to discover my part.

Recently a group of people from my church conducted a campaign against the ministers. The predictable outcome was greater anger and division. It caused me to take another look at my own anger issues.

Here is a simple truth. My husband is a wonderful person who happens to be a bit of a slob. He typically leaves a mess in the kitchen. He will leave food scraps in the sink around the garbage disposal. Surely it would be simple to turn on the water and flip the switch.

One day I can see a mess and feel enraged. Another day I see the same mess and see an opportunity to do something loving. Still other times I see the same mess and realize he will probably clean it up when he gets around to it, or I can clean it up now for myself. How I feel has nothing whatsoever to do with his actions. I am free to feel whatever emotion shows up, or I am free to change how I feel.

Nicotine Anonymous freed me from the prison of my addiction, and taught me how to free myself from the illusion of fear and anger.

Today, I am free to accept conflict
as an opportunity for discovery.

> Patience is something you admire in the driver
> behind you, but not in the one ahead.
>
> —BILL MCGLASHEN

I believed patience was a virtue for others not for me. Patient people never accomplished anything. One day a few years ago I came up with the perfect answer for patience. I could prove I was patient because I was willing to wait for my next lifetime to work on patience.

Nevertheless, opportunities for patience continued to bombard me until I decided to investigate that attribute. I bought a book about the power of patience and decided to give that virtue a try.

I remembered admiring people who take on time-consuming difficult jobs and then calmly proceed to accomplish them. I realized how many tasks or hobbies I avoided because it would take too much time. I thought of all the tension I have felt waiting in lines or behind slow drivers. I get enraged because things were not going well with some task, but if I stop I realize things are not working because I am hungry and tired. When I take care of the hunger and rest the task becomes simple.

In the past, I used nicotine to keep me going, to push aside any demands my body was making. Without nicotine, I am learning how to successfully deal with life. I am getting far more than just freedom from nicotine.

Today, I will stop and check in with
myself when I am feeling the need to
HALT ("Hungry, Angry, Lonely, Tired").

Awareness releases reality to change you.

—ANTHONY DE MELLO

One Sunday my minister was talking about strength and using dandelions as her example. Does the survival come from the puff ball of seeds children and the wind love to blow, or from the amazing root system?

Visiting Scotland one year I was sitting outside a museum and noticed one dandelion in the meticulously kept green lawn. Inspired by the flower and the earlier sermon, I painted a simple portrait of dandelions. It hangs in my office.

One day using the painting as a meditation aid, I realized what both the minister and I had previously missed, the leaves. How do you kill dandelions? You continuously cut off the leaves. Eventually the root system will die.

The Twelve Steps have given me a fuller richer life through the practice of prayer and meditation. I am gaining a greater appreciation for every aspect of life. As I grow in loving unconditionally I am better able to appreciate the tremendous diversity of personalities and talents of humanity.

Today, I will look for the beauty and strength of someone very different from me.

A loving heart is the truest wisdom.

—CHARLES DICKENS

Accountability continues to be an issue for me. My son's drug addiction pushed me through the door of a Twelve Step Program. I heard him and the other adolescents in his group talk about holding each other accountable. The question for me has been to find the line between holding someone accountable and taking someone else's inventory.

When someone starts saying something blaming about a mutual acquaintance, do I just listen, providing a shoulder to cry on? Or do I suggest they first look within themselves for their part?

Sometimes I am able to simply acknowledge the other person's hurt. I may even be able to relate a personal similar experience when I later could look at my part. The absolute hardest thing for me to do is to not try to fix the other person or situation.

Today, I will be alert to indications I am
trying to fix some other person.

In nature we never expect to see a rose without
thorns, nor spring without winter, not even
a cow without dung.
—AMAN MOTWANE

My first sponsor asked me to redo my Fourth Step when I did
my initial Fifth Step. She suggested a specific format that
would allow me to simplify the process.

I revised the Fourth Step, but she still wanted more. She asked me to
go back, using the revised Fourth Step as a guide. She wanted me to find
the strength behind each character defect.

What a revelation. I discovered that every single defect was the flip
side of a particular strength. Then I could understand that the defects
were just using strengths to extreme. I realized I did not have to abandon
my personality, becoming a completely different person. I just had to
learn to recognize when I was going overboard. I just had to look for the
proper balance.

Today, I will view discomfort
as a call to look for balance.

Forgiveness is the giving,
so the receiving of life.
—GEORGE MACDONALD

When I came into this Program, I started hearing about boundaries. I had no clue what boundaries were, what boundaries I should establish, or how to avoid crossing other's boundaries.

I found a great pamphlet on boundaries, but I would get lost trying to study it. Gradually I started to catch on. I started to realize that I could define my boundaries by feelings of anger or hurt.

Still further in my recovery, I could acknowledge that my boundaries could and would change over time and in response to various circumstances. I started understanding that I would not always agree with someone else's boundaries, and that others would not always respond lovingly to my boundaries. I realized I alone have responsibility for defining and communicating my boundaries. I will not blame someone else for violating a boundary I have not communicated. I will simply explain my position.

Today, I take responsibility for my own
boundaries, and I acknowledge the right of
others to have their own.

Everyone has the right to choose what he or she
says and does. A relationship is the natural result
of people making independent choices.

—GREG BAER

In a study group, one person talked about the importance of
accountability. She talked about what that meant to her. Her
comments resonated with me particularly in connection with my
relationship to her. Later, privately, I discussed it with her further.

I needed clarification from her about how she wanted to be treated.
This particular person was in a position of high visibility and great
influence. At various times she had made disparaging comments about
others to me or in front of me. What I heard from the private discussion
was that I simply did not have to welcome or encourage any negativity,
rather than pointing out to the other person their character defects. I
accepted that as her boundary.

Later she came under intense fire from others for her past actions. I
did not make myself available to participate in the emails and
conversations criticizing her, so I do not really know what others were
saying. From comments people made directly to me, I believe her
transgression were probably greatly exaggerated. I do know that she
suffered tremendously.

Because I honored her boundary, I was in the position to love her
and to love those who attacked her. I did not have to take sides.

---

*Today, I will honor others' right to establish
boundaries whether or not I agree
with the boundaries.*

> If you change your perception, you change the
> experience of your body and your world.
>
> —DEEPAK CHOPRA

My first sponsor always introduced herself in meetings as a real nicotine addict. At some point in her comments, she always talked about living "life on life's terms." I was amused at the idea she was a real nicotine addict, because her level of addiction, or perhaps her bottom did not seem that extreme to me.

Her commitment to live "life on life's terms" was always important to me. I needed nicotine because I refused to live that way. Under stress I turned to nicotine rather than looking for a way to lower my stress level. I used nicotine to medicate my feelings, but once the nicotine wore off the feelings were still there.

Nicotine Anonymous has shown me the wisdom of facing feelings without my drug. Only then can I decide how best to deal with the person or situation. I changed my career because without nicotine I really hated doing most of the tasks my position required.

Today, I will live "life on life's terms."

Fear defeats more people than any other
one thing in the world.
—RALPH WALDO EMERSON

I wish I knew how to get in touch with some of the people I met early in my recovery from nicotine addiction. Here is one story about a person who has been a great influence for me.

She came for the first time a week after I joined. She stood in the doorway, not at all sure whether she should come in, but with encouragement she finally did. That was exactly how I felt the first time. I was scared to death the Program would work, and I was scared it would not work.

Anonymity was vital to her because she had just started a job and had claimed to be a non-smoker in her interview. That was a job requirement. Now she had to find a way to quit.

In calling her at work one day, another member identified himself as a friend from Nicotine Anonymous. She felt betrayed and quit coming to our group. Anonymity had never been important to me because everyone knew I was an addict. That incident made me aware of how vital that Tradition is to some of our members. When asked how I know someone from a Twelve Step Program I say we met through mutual friends.

*Today, I honor each person's
right to anonymity.*

Everything has been figured out
except how to live.

—JEAN-PAUL SARTRE

When I first started I made the decision to make attending meetings my highest priority. I let my boss know I had to attend meetings on Tuesday and Thursday night, and could not work too late. He really wanted me to quit so he was willing to accept any delay in getting work completed.

After I had quit and had some time in recovery, I realized my life had been chaos. I could never plan my evenings without being willing to abandon my plans. He was notorious about pushing deadlines then having everyone around him jump through hoops to get projects out on time.

After I quit medicating my feelings, he wanted me to stay late one night, but I had other plans. My sister was passing through town and we just had time for dinner before she caught the last flight out. My boss came up with an emergency project minutes before I was to leave. He could not stay because his son had a soccer game, so he wanted me to cancel my plans.

I refused to change my plans. I finally understood I am entitled to make and keep plans that are important to me. I do not have to justify their importance to others.

*Today, I can set a boundary or be flexible
according to my own needs and desires.*

Experience keeps a dear school, but
fools will learn in no other.

—BENJAMIN FRANKLIN

In the first weeks of my recovery another newcomer helped me understand the lengths I would go to feed my addiction. Once when she was quitting, she decided to limit the number of cigarettes. She had done that before unsuccessfully, so she came up with a different plan.

She put her cigarettes and lighter in her attic. To get to her attic, she had to open her garage door, back her car out of the garage, pull down the ladder, climb up and get and light one cigarette. Climb back down, push the ladder and door back up, pull the car back in and close the garage door. The first day she smoked the whole pack then abandoned the strategy.

Once when I was trying to quit, I decided to lock my cigarettes and lighter in my car. To get one, I would have to leave my condo, cross a cat walk, wait for the elevator down, walk across the parking lot, unlock my car, then unlock the glove compartment. Then I would relock the glove box and car, walk back across the parking lot, in through the first locked door to the lobby with the elevator, go up, cross back over the cat walk, unlock the second door to the hall, then walk down the hall to my unit. After my sixth trip, I took the cigarettes and lighter back up with me.

*Today, I am free of the insanity of
trying to break free of my addiction.*

I love being married. It's so great to
find that one special person you want
to annoy for the rest of your life.
—RITA RUDNER

I remember helping plan for my parents' twenty-fifth wedding anniversary. Mom wanted a big celebration because she was convinced Dad would not live long enough to celebrate their fiftieth. Dad had the common twin addictions of alcohol and nicotine.

Somehow he survived to their fiftieth anniversary, and it was time for another big party. Mom could not find just the right dress, so she had one made, something she had never done before. Days before the party the dress was ready, but it did not fit and it looked terrible on her. She had a friend who had been a dressmaker, but had quit and was very involved in other endeavors. With no time to even shop for another dress, she called the friend. The friend worked her magic and the dress was saved.

A rain storm blew in just before the party, and even using an umbrella, the lower portion of the dress got wet, and the fabric puckered badly. She finally gave up and decided to focus on the real purpose of the day.

How many times have I done something similar? I can get so caught up in plans that I lose sight of my purpose.

*Today, I will pause periodically to get back in
touch with the purpose behind my activities.*

We do not see things as they are;
we see things as we are.
—TALMUD

One day a woman walked into my convenience store and went into the restroom. She stayed in there for thirty minutes while others gave up waiting. Before she emerged I had gotten irritated then worried. I was not thinking kind thoughts by the time she left, particularly because she had not bought anything at all. Even worse, she left the sink clogged and the plumber discovered a mass of hair in the trap.

Perhaps a year later, a woman walked into the store and asked to speak privately with me. She wanted to thank me. She let me know she had been homeless, and used the store's restroom to bathe and wash her hair before a job interview. She got the job and was able to pay for a home for herself and her children.

Here I had judged her as a thoughtless, inconsiderate person, when she was a loving mother desperate to find a way to take care of her children and herself. Suddenly the cost of the plumber seemed insignificant.

Today, I am willing to look for
only the good in others.

People only see what they
are prepared to see.

—RALPH WALDO EMERSON

L ike a lot of people in the post 9-11 economy I was underemployed. I had a part time job paying less than my monthly expenses. I stopped by the grocery store just before Christmas on a bitterly cold day. I was wearing my full-length tourmaline mink coat so I certainly gave the appearance of prosperity.

A woman with a baby in a stroller approached me in the parking lot asking for money for groceries. My normal reaction would have been to just turn her down or suggest that she accompany me inside, pick out groceries and pay for them. Instead, I took out my wallet and gave her all the money inside, less than twenty dollars. Then I drove to the bank ATM and took out more money.

I felt gloriously prosperous. I could casually give away all the money I had with me, and just go get more. I had been making a deliberate attempt each day to release concerns about tomorrow's needs and simply see if I had everything I need for this moment. I always found that I did.

Today, I will take care of
just this moment.

The way we see things is the source of the
way we think and the way we act.

—STEPHEN COVEY

Appearances are important to me. I went to great lengths to look good, and smoking was not acceptable. I would get up each morning before anyone else so I could sneak outside for a couple of cigarettes. Then I would come in and get my children up and off to school. Before I got ready for work, I would sneak outside again.

At lunch time I would race home, take off my clothes, put on a robe, and wrap a towel around my head so I could have a couple of more cigarettes. Then I would brush my teeth, get dressed and go back to work.

Even though I went to great lengths to hide my smoking, I still managed to smoke over a pack a day. To some people that might not seem like a lot, but it certainly consumed a tremendous amount of my time and energy, and I just could not quit.

I found my way to Nicotine Anonymous and freedom. Thanks to this Program, I am learning to allow my outsides to match my insides. I have made the decision to quit sneaking around doing things that cause me shame.

Today, I thank God I no longer
have to sneak around.

> Even if you're on the right track, you'll get run
> over if you just sit there.
>
> —WILL ROGERS

I used to think I was a mistake. It did not seem as though I had any real purpose for existing. I spent most of my life trying to work harder and smarter than others to justify taking up valuable earth resources. My worthiness was based purely on what I could accomplish rather than on who I am.

Then I found my way to Nicotine Anonymous. You loved me for who I am, not for what I could do. Without nicotine, I had to learn to look at myself and find out who I really am, what excites me, what gives me joy. I even changed the direction of my career.

Still today I find myself questioning my life and looking back. I talk with people who do jobs that I used to do and I am tempted to find a job more like I used to have. Then I have to remember the whole of my past, not just the highs. My job used to consume all my energy. I used to be an adrenalin junkie. Give me a crisis and enough nicotine and I could work miracles. I now have time and energy for hobbies and community service, and I know I really do not want to give those up.

Today, I will direct my thoughts
forward in a positive direction.

I know God promises not to give me more than I can
handle. I just wish He didn't trust me so much.

—MOTHER TERESA

After some time working the Twelve Steps I realized that I have a
unique purpose in life. Whether I fulfill that purpose or not is up
to me, but no one else has that specific purpose; no one else
could do it just the way I do.

A friend conducted a workshop on discovering and defining your
personal life mission. I went hoping to leave with some mission other
than the one I had identified. Instead I just left with a concise mission
statement. It was too big and it scared me. To accomplish my mission it
seemed as though I would have to give up everything else and devote
myself full time.

Finally during meditation I realized the great truth. My mission is
mine because it is what I do naturally as I go about my daily life.
Knowing my mission gives me a yardstick. When I am tempted by some
new venture or activity, I can pull out my yardstick and see if the activity
would further my mission or be a diversion. I can still choose a diversion,
but I understand that is what I am choosing.

*Today, I can make choices
with clarity.*

I might not have gone where I intended to go, but I think I have ended up where I intended to be.

—DOUGLAS ADAMS

It is amazing that I could for years understand that I was addicted to nicotine and be vaguely aware of the Twelve Steps without ever understanding the unmanageability part of Step One. From my first experience with nicotine to my last, my life was unmanageable in some way.

Early in my nicotine life I drove with my younger sister to visit our older sister who had moved out of state and recently had a baby. We had a great visit. She and her husband had just one car and he drove it to work most days, leaving her at home or on foot with the young baby. He had decided she should quit smoking so he would not get her any cigarettes. It was about two miles to the nearest store.

On the drive home my ashtray was full and a cigarette did not get put all the way out causing a filter to smolder. My sister was not getting it put out so I diverted my attention from driving to putting out the filter. I had a wreck. The car turned completely over and then end to end before landing on its side in a ditch.

It is not as though there were not ample evidence of unmanageability, but I could not see it.

Today, I will look at life with my eyes wide open and recognize evidence of unmanageability.

> There is nothing like returning to a place that
> remains unchanged to find the ways in which
> you yourself have altered.
>
> —NELSON MANDELLA

How I treasure newcomers. They do indeed remind me of the progress I have made thanks to the Twelve Steps. Formerly I was shy, always working diligently to support others; today I am a dynamic public speaker. I used to be insecure and prone to look for evidence others were no better than I; now I am free to look for the good in every person, including myself. I believed I was attracted to mates who had a problem with intimacy; I learned I was the one afraid to let others too close because of what they might find.

I used to envy others' talents; now I use any such thoughts as an indication of a talent longing to be expressed by me. I used to think those who rushed out of the office promptly at the end of the normal work day lacked dedication; I have learned honoring myself makes me a better employee. I used to be so conscious of the need to do things correctly that I avoided taking chances; today I know a failure is just an opportunity to try a different approach.

This list could go on forever. It is amazing how I have changed, and become more my true self through this Fellowship.

Today, I will be aware if I say, "one of these days, I will . . . " and see what action I can take right now.

> God loves you not because you are good. No,
> God loves you, period. God loves us not because
> we are lovable. No, we are lovable precisely
> because God loves us.
>
> —DESMOND TUTU

The greatest gift of Twelve Step Programs is unconditional love. It is truly amazing to me that I can listen to someone share a character defect, share a story of some time they behaved in a way for which they feel guilt and shame, and I can see the lovable human in the speaker. In my family of origin I could not tolerate those same actions.

Not immediately, only very gradually I could begin to see certain family members as normal human beings. As humans they and I do not always behave lovingly and rationally. This Program has allowed me to see my part in past events and to release resentments that had kept me chained to past hurts. This Program has also taught me to make amends when I am all too human.

Today, I will pause and ask what the most
loving response would be before I
automatically voice my thoughts.

There is a wisdom of the head,
and a wisdom of the heart.

—CHARLES DICKENS

Sometimes I am willing, or at least I believe that I am, to release resentment long before my heart finally lets go and moves on. Recently my church community had a period of serious turmoil that lead to the resignation of our ministers. My first thought was if they leave, I am leaving, but one minister reminded me of all the people I would leave behind. Then many of those who were important to me left anyway.

I do not agree with the method those dissatisfied chose to employ, although I do honor their right to express anger and hurt. I ultimately decided to stay to be an instrument of peace and healing. Over the past few years I have become increasingly interested in constructive ways to deal with conflict. Having made the decision to be peace and healing, I had to back up intention with action. That meant releasing resentment against those who pushed their angry agenda.

I would think I had made great emotional progress, then see one person for the first time and find the resentment was still strong. Thanks to the Twelve Steps I was able to be the leader I wanted to be. These Steps are so very powerful applied to everyday life.

Today, I will reaffirm rational decisions until my heart catches up with my head.

> Let your religion be less of a theory
> and more of a love affair.
> —GILBERT K. CHESTERTON

If I substitute the phrase "spiritual awareness" for the word "religion" this has more relevance for me. I do not remain nicotine-free by trying to use the Twelve Steps just for nicotine addiction. I have to practice the principles in all my affairs.

Whenever I find myself in distress I go back to Step One. I admit I am powerless over the person or situation, and I get in touch with exactly how my life has become unmanageable. I may find myself angry. I may have trouble sleeping. I may be gaining weight. I may find that little irritations make me enraged.

Once I get through Step One, I know how to continue taking each next Step. I personally have to make the decision and effort to go all the way back to Step One, and not try to race to a later Step.

Today, I agree to take the Steps, one at a
time, in the appropriate order.

I prayed for twenty years but received no
answer until I prayed with my legs.
—FREDERICK DOUGLASS

I would like to say this quote does not apply to me. I thought I prayed
with my legs for years before I found my way to Nicotine
Anonymous. I quit using every conceivable trick and method anyone
suggested, some more that once. I just never stayed quit.

If I am honest, I have to admit that I never really quit; I only
conditionally quit. Sooner or later some person or situation would make
me start again.

This Fellowship makes me get honest. No one or circumstance can
make me use nicotine; that is a choice I make. I can use the Steps and this
Program to deal with "life on life's terms"; or I can go back to my drug.

*Today, I will use gratitude to get me
back on the right path.*

> The price of anything is the amount of
> life you exchange for it.
>
> —HENRY DAVID THOREAU

The price of anything suggests a cost; the value of anything suggests the return on the investment. The value of recovery from my nicotine addiction is priceless. The actual price I paid was the commitment to attend every Nicotine Anonymous meeting in my area, no matter what. There were times it was inconvenient, but I would compare the inconvenience to the effort I would have been willing to make to get my drug.

I never had to go out in the middle of the night and drive on icy streets to get to a meeting. I never had to lie and sneak out of my work. I never had to use grocery money. I gave up bronchitis. I gave up standing out in the cold and rain. I gave up lectures from doctors, friends and family.

Anytime I thought a meeting was too inconvenient, I would think of another member. He lost his job and wound up having to temporarily live with his sister who lived sixty-five or more miles from the meeting. He still made meetings.

Today, I am grateful for
the priceless gift of recovery.

Write injuries in dust,
benefits in marble
—BENJAMIN FRANKLIN

Sometimes I have been astounded to learn that I have hurt someone else's feelings. There have been times when someone thought I said something I really never said. The other day I said, "I haven't" and my husband thought I said, "I have it." That started a conversation, and I thought he was hearing things because I had not said anything remotely like what he thought I said. Finally I repeated exactly what I had said and he figured out the difference.

Whether someone actually says something or I believe they have said something the impact can be identical. This Program has given me the tools to be honest with the person about what I heard and how I felt, and allows the other person the chance to correct any misunderstanding. Before the Twelve Steps, I would have just brooded and misjudged the person. When I can handle relationships in this manner, it opens the door for others to do the same.

*Today, I will be honest in communications
and be open to the possibility I have
misunderstood or been misunderstood.*

Aim at heaven and you will get earth thrown in.
Aim at earth and you get neither.
—C. S. LEWIS

There are a lot of versions of this idea. To me it means that I use the Twelve Steps to the best of my ability. Sometimes I will do fine; other times I will miss the mark and land with a thud having hurt someone's feelings.

Step Ten reminds me to continue to take a personal inventory. If I notice any indication of a strain in a relationship I can ask the other person if there is any problem or if I have done anything that hurt their feelings. It is never my intention to hurt another. I can always be genuinely contrite if something I did or said caused discomfort to another.

Making amends does not mean I am bad or that I was wrong in what I said or did. I have not given up the right to disagree with others, sometimes very strongly. Sometimes making amends is just acknowledging the other person's right to have a different position.

Today, I will be sensitive to others' feelings, and apologize promptly if I land in the mud.

Faith is spiritualized imagination.

—HENRY WARD BEECHER

Scientists have been trying to prove or disprove the concept of God for centuries. Philosophers have been debating the issue. But no one has concrete evidence either way. It takes faith in a Power greater than ourselves, not proof.

I seriously and diligently tried every means in my control to break free of my compulsion to use nicotine, but was unsuccessful. Our Fellowship provided the strength I lacked. Not only do we provide each other the ability to get and stay free, we help each other learn to live better lives.

To me the efforts human beings have consistently made over centuries in becoming better people are evidence of a greater Power.

Today, I will look for the good in every person.

DECEMBER 10

Life is a dance. Am I dancing?

—UNKNOWN

Am I enjoying life? Am I trying to enjoy life? Am I giving myself a break and practicing, "easy does it" on myself and other people?

I believe God wants me to be "happy, joyous and free." I believe God wants me to live free of addiction and at times dance to the music I feel inside. I believe God wants me to help others dance to the sounds of their own music.

And if I am not careful I am inclined to be too busy to dance and enjoy life as I was when I was feeding my nicotine addiction.

Today, I thank God for helping me enjoy this precious gift of life.

I always pretended that it was no big deal to be around
non-smokers, but it was a total pain in the ass.
—NICOTINE ANONYMOUS: THE BOOK

How true for me. It got so I would avoid going places with
non-smokers because it interfered with my smoking. And that
included most of the population out there, eventually even
including my girlfriend.

Things are different now. After I quit smoking I thought it was cool
to hang out with people who were smoking. I try to avoid this now. I am
still a smoker in recovery and I do not need to be around people who are
actively smoking. I like the smell of tobacco too much.

So I avoid bars and other places where people smoke, not completely
but mostly. And I always try to be compassionate toward smokers and
other nicotine addicts and give them their right to live as they are living.

I am grateful to live in a time and place where the rights of
non-smokers are so great. I remember the days we were allowed to
smoke everywhere except church and elevators, and I even lit up once or
twice in elevators.

*Today, I will be tolerant of others
regardless of our differences.*

A man who carries a cat by the tail learns
something he can learn in no other way.

—MARK TWAIN

My selfishness is the root of my troubles, before and after recovery. I was such a selfish smoker, expecting non-smokers to accept my smoke in their air. I was irritated when a friend put a sign asking people not to smoke in her work area, thinking how selfish she was. I was angry when the company eventually banned smoking from the workplace except in designated areas. My brother is still this way, and it drives me away from him now that I am free of tobacco.

In recovery I see in my Step Ten inventories my selfishness is still very much with me. It comes out in fear, self-pity, jealously, and many other ways. And yes, subtly when I step on the toes of my fellows they retaliate in their own ways, if only to steer clear of me.

*Today, I will ask God to relieve me of the bondage
of self and allow me to be of loving service.*

> One may know how to gain a victory,
> and know not how to use it.
> —PEDRO CALDERON DE LA BARCA

All those wasted years I smoked from my teens into my late forties. It was inevitable for me as the child of two heavy smokers. I lived in the lie of believing that smoking tobacco was helping me live a better life, at such a high cost in so many ways that only smokers understand. So many wasted feelings numbed with the drug nicotine.

Thank God for our Twelve Steps and Fellowship to guide me away from my drug and toward each other and God. After almost nine years of living free of nicotine, I know with certainty this is the best way to live, free from addiction and living with God as I understand God, trying to "do the next right thing."

Today, I am grateful for smobriety and being able to share this precious life.

Never give up, for that is just the place
and time the tide will turn.

—HARRIET BEECHER STOWE

I read the *Bible* for strength, hope and encouragement. Exodus 14:14 says, "The Lord shall fight for you and you shall hold your place." This is so great for me because cigarettes were a sedative. When I know someone cares this much it is very soothing.

I now have eight months without nicotine. It is so rewarding. I did not feel real well yet, but I hiked for two miles with a group knowing oxygenating my blood would be beneficial. It was a great hiking party. I would not have done that as a smoker.

*Today, I will take time to
enjoy healthy activities.*

The door to wisdom
is never shut.

—BENJAMIN FRANKLIN

I believe with all my heart and soul that God is doing for me what I could not do for myself to allow me to live free of addiction and do so much more in my life.

When I was a teenager, around age sixteen, I started using nicotine and about the same time quit going to church and praying. I decided I did not believe in the church I was raised in and almost subconsciously threw out believing in God. I gave up God and figured I could live by my own power. This proved to be a huge mistake. I did not realize I could give up the human church and go directly to God.

This mistake cost me dearly with years of chemical addiction, depression, suicidal negativity and wasted years.

I am so grateful that the Twelve Steps, people in recovery, and God brought me back to a spiritual path. I feel the power of my Higher Power and my faith in service and kindness.

Today, I dance to God's songs
of gratitude and joy and living
"one day at a time" free of addiction.

Even if one glimpses God, there are still cuts and
splinters and burns.... No wall or avoidance or denial
can keep the rawness of life from running through us.

—MARK NEPO

There are some days when the best I can do is make it through the
day without using nicotine. There are days when after eight years
of recovery I feel so raw and burned I feel like nothing is worth
anything. Then by the grace of God I bounce back and feel grateful and
healed and ready to go.

I am grateful those bad days are short-lived. In the addiction period
of my life those dark clouds would cover me for weeks or months or
years, with suicidal storms passing through. Since recovery and
practicing the Twelve Steps I have a daily reprieve from the worst of it.

But I still get those days. Sharing with my home groups in recovery,
my sponsor, and God helps pull me out of the negativity which seems so
familiar to me. I am reminded that the rawness of life runs through me at
times and that is OK, to be accepted and embraced as the way life is for
me. Was I trying to run away from life's fullness when I was using
nicotine?

*Today, I am grateful to live free of addiction, truly
experiencing all of life and enjoying the adventure.*

Prayer is not asking. It is a longing of the soul. It is daily
admission of one's weakness ... it is better in prayer to have a
heart without words than words without a heart.

—MOHANDAS GHANDI

My most sincere and heartfelt prayer is, "Thank you God." It is
gratitude.

Yes, I pray with many words and express desires, fears and
feelings other than gratitude. Those prayers share the theme of "please
help me." They are genuinely felt prayers, admissions of my weakness,
and I believe they are heard by God. But nowhere do I feel that sense of
sincerity other than in praying, "Thank you God for this life to share
with You here in this moment."

Prayer and meditation are so solidly recommended by the Twelve
Steps. They are my bridges to know God. I cannot thus far in my
recovery let go of the more selfish prayers but in meditation I reach out
to God for anything that comes.

---

*Today, I will add prayers of gratitude
to any cries for help.*

Like life itself, the Steps
are a process and a cycle.

—NICOTINE ANONYMOUS: THE BOOK

A friend in recovery likes to describe the Steps as a circle that goes round and round, and can go either way depending on what is needed. I see so much progress at times in my life, and so much frustration at other times, even after many years of recovery.

I like the hammer; it works pretty well, but it can sure cause a lot of damage if used the wrong way. So what are the tools of the Program?

Having a sponsor and trusted friends in recovery I can be really honest with and not fear they will use my truth against me. This is so important, having a group or more than one group where I can reveal what is truly going on with me.

Not trying to use my group as a hunting ground for sexual or business purposes is very important for me, no matter how tempting that is at times.

Having a close, intimate, genuine relationship with a Higher Power I call God is so important in my recovery.

Trying to live life the way I believe God wants me to live and trying to promptly correct the wrongs I do.

Relying on and trusting that God has my best interests in mind, even though I do not know what that entails.

I can reach out to other people in recovery and share my "experience, strength and hope." I volunteer to be of service, and reach out to new people with their inevitable struggles and lack of understanding. I practice recovery principles with everyone, including myself.

*Today, I am grateful for the many tools
and practices of our Program.*

Life is like playing a violin solo in public and
learning the instrument as one goes on.

—SAMUEL BUTLER

I have felt incomplete most of my life, always in the process of
learning and growing, struggling for the day when I would be good
enough. I felt like there was a true me hiding in the depths.

I am reminded of the story of Alfred Wallace the naturalist who
could no longer bear to watch the struggle of a moth trying to break out
of the cocoon so he gently split the cocoon with a knife, only to watch
the moth die because it had not developed the strength it needed to live.

When the caterpillar is crawling around it is fully itself, not just a
moth in waiting. Later as a chrysalis in the cocoon it is still perfectly the
creature it is meant to be.

The quiet child of my past was fully and truly me, the person I
needed to have the experiences to develop into the person I am today.
Unlike the caterpillar, I can imagine who I might be in the future. That
does not mean who I am today is not whole and complete.

*Today, I will learn from the caterpillar to love
myself in every stage of my being.*

Made a decision to turn our will and our lives over
to the care of God as we understood Him.
—STEP THREE

In this Step I am making a decision to take the rest of the Steps using the Power I identified in Step Two. Once again, this Power can come from Nicotine Anonymous, my Nicotine Anonymous sponsor or any way I choose to view God. There are even atheistic views of this Power. The primary theme of this Step is the removal of self, and the replacing of it with the recovery outlined in Steps Four through Twelve. When I take this Step, I can take it with a fellow Nicotine Anonymous member, or my sponsor or a loved one. I often say the Third Step Prayer to signify that I have made the decision to recover.

"Relieve me of the bondage of self. Help me abandon myself to the spirit. Move me to do good in this world and show kindness. Help me to overcome and avoid anger, resentment, jealousy and any other kind of negative thinking today. Help me to help those who suffer. Keep me alert with courage to face life and not withdraw from it, not to insulate myself from all pain whereby I insulate myself from love as well. Free me from fantasy and fear. Inspire and direct my thinking today; let it be divorced from self-pity, dishonesty and self-seeking motives. Show me the way of patience, tolerance kindliness and love. I pray for all of those to whom I've been unkind and ask that they are granted the same peace that I seek."

After having taken this Step, I do not dwell on my decision, nor do I hesitate. I move right into my personal housecleaning; Steps Four through Nine.

*Today, I will remind myself that removal of my
self is the only effective method for recovery.*

Show up, pay attention, tell the truth and don't be
attached to the outcome.

—ANGELES ARRIEN

As the winter solstice approaches and the days become shorter, I am reminded of the darkness that seemed to grip me with increasing strength in the final days of my active addiction: the social ostracism; the fear, anxiety and worry over the harm I was causing myself physically; the utter hopelessness I felt about ever being able to quit.

I feared living without my constant companion. I anticipated that life without nicotine would be impossible. But the solstice teaches me that this projection was unwarranted. Just when it seems the darkness will never end, there comes a turning point when the days become longer and warmer. Just as I anticipated that life would be unbearable without nicotine, recovery teaches me that life can filled with so much goodness, beyond my wildest dreams.

*Today, I choose to live in anticipation that light
inevitably follows darkness.*

The wind of God's grace is always blowing, but
you must raise your sails.

—VIVEKANANDA

A fter almost thirty years of smoking cigarettes, I finally realized I
was insane. This enlightenment came to me one morning at
six a.m. as I lit my first smoke of the day. I had been awakened at
four a.m. once again, coughing so hard I could barely catch my breath.
And here I was, two hours later, smoking a cigarette. Insanity.

Divine guidance led me to a counselor. I told him how I had come to
the realization that I was insane, and in reply he handed me a copy of
Nicotine Anonymous: The Book. I realized that I was being asked to
"walk the walk," instead of just talking the talk. I admitted that I was an
addict to nicotine, I was powerless over my addiction, and that my life
had become unmanageable.

I have not used nicotine since December 22, 2000. People
congratulated me and praised me for my willpower. My willpower was
not strong enough; my willpower had been losing the battle with my
addiction for years. Only when I surrendered my will to my Higher
Power was I graced with freedom from the chains of my addiction.

*Today, I am willing to listen to my Higher Power,
and to act as I am guided.*

> People who are cocky and arrogant say, I know
> that" and move along. People who are confident
> and positive ask themselves, "how good am I at
> that?" and seek to improve.
>
> —JEFFREY GITOMER

In Nicotine Anonymous, nicotine is often referred to as our "lower power," the power we turned to time and time again to self-medicate to feel good physically, mentally, and emotionally. Now through this gentle Program of Nicotine Anonymous and the Twelve Steps, we learn to turn to a Higher Power to help us stay nicotine-free.

For me, nicotine was the glue that held my brain, thinking, feelings, and life together for twenty-five years. Without it, even a few months without it, my life feels like a jigsaw puzzle with the pieces scattered all about. I do not know how the pieces fit together. Only my Higher Power can see the bigger picture. My Higher Power will be the "super glue" that will hold me together when I feel like I am falling apart.

Today, when things seem crazy and hard to understand, I can take a deep breath, relax, and know a greater hand has things under control.

We must so live that, when it comes time to die,
even the undertaker is sorry.

—MARK TWAIN

When I first came to Nicotine Anonymous, a Promise was read to me that I will realize I haven't given up anything at all. I did not believe this as I knew I was giving up something huge. I was quitting because I knew if I kept doing the crime that eventually I was going to have to do the time. I did not want to do time with cancer, heart disease, emphysema, so it was worth giving up my little friends.

In fact they were not my friends. I have gained so much by getting freedom from addiction and I now know the Promises are true. I was slowing dying. Now I am living.

Today, I will pause and give thanks for the realization of the Promises in my life.

> Time is the longest distance
> between two places.
> —TENNESSEE WILLIAMS

How many New Year's resolutions came and went until I finally found Nicotine Anonymous? How many quit dates passed? Birthdays, holidays, Mondays, any days until I was ready to be willing, until I watched people who had what I wanted, freedom from nicotine, I could not get freed of this powerful addiction.

And what I heard at meetings was not about not giving up nicotine forever. Instead I heard about just not feeding my addiction "one day at a time." This was a totally new approach for me, and it seemed much more attractive and manageable than forever. It still does after celebrating five years free. I am so grateful for this Program, "one day at a time."

"Just for today," I choose not to use nicotine. I will worry about tomorrow some other time.

DECEMBER 26

The man who makes no mistakes
does not usually make anything.
—WILLIAM CONNOR MAGEE

As a newcomer I was so terrified of what Nicotine Anonymous
members would think of me if I "did something wrong." But no
matter what I did or said, all they had in response was a warm,
friendly, "keep coming back."

I keep myself miserable by my fear of making mistakes. Since I have
learned to love myself, right or wrong, I make a lot more mistakes than
ever before, and I have a lot more successes.

*Today, I know that I never fail
when I give my best effort.*

The best way to escape from your problem
is to solve it.
—ROBERT ANTHONY

Relationships challenge me. For years I have isolated myself from others, although I was not too aware that I did. I even appeared smooth and lively, at times the life of the party.

Inside, I was often dying to escape, to get away from all these people. An inner pressure would build up in me that made me just want to run away to be alone. Lately, that inner pressure seems less extreme. When it is building up, I try to stop my thoughts and figure out what is bothering me. If I am honest, I can usually find the source of my tension. Just recognizing the real problem seems to reduce its power for me.

If I am uncomfortable at this moment, do not be concerned. In a little while I will be okay. If I use nicotine, I will not be any better off, but I may well wind up enslaved again for the rest of my days.

I may push people away from me just because I want them so much I cannot stand the tension. I may want their approval, or fear their anger, or need their attention.

---

*Today, if I feel pressure, I will stop and
determine the source of my discomfort. Then
I will be prepared to address that need.*

> All these activities help us develop different paths of
> ourselves, to bring more clarity, compassion, and self-
> awareness, to attain the highest level of who we are. In
> turn, we are able to share this with others.
> —NICOTINE ANONYMOUS MEMBER

So many good thoughts are shared at meetings. Who could speak
more pointedly to my nicotine-affected life than another addict?
One poetic member explained how the struggle to quit felt to her
in these words, "God and the Devil were arguing in my head, and I was
rooting for the Devil."

She was an honest person. She knew the choice to quit was not a
clear and easy decision. Even so when the urge hits, I now have choices. I
do not have to choose nicotine.

I am fortunate to have the support and guidance available at
meetings. I get the benefit of this support by getting myself out to
meetings. Sometimes when I least feel like going, the meeting is the most
beneficial for me. When I am feeling less needy, I can go to meetings to
give to new members the help and support that was given to me.
Meetings sustain me through the most difficult stages of getting free from
nicotine. I discover the depths that the Program offers in shaping a better
way of life where I can grow beyond addiction.

Today, I am grateful for my new life with clarity,
compassion and self-awareness.

How much more grievous are the consequences
of anger than the causes of it.
—MARCUS AURELIUS

Anger simmers inside me, boiling up at times. It is hurting the wrong people, coming out at the wrong time, and causing me problems. Did I quit using nicotine to become a monster? Where is this anger coming from?

Until recently, I buried my feelings by distracting myself with tobacco. Now I am dealing with a backlog of emotional energy that has never been acknowledged.

It is true that I have taken the lid off my emotions. Things will be turbulent for a time, but with each experience I gain some self-knowledge. If a certain thing has irritated me for a long time, now I can look at that and examine the best way to deal with my discomfort. If I blow up, timely apologies can mend the hurt of my hasty words. I discover that I must learn to guard my words when I am upset. I am gaining control over my emotional reactions. Each of these lessons moves me along the road to emotional recovery. That is one of the many gifts of getting free from the nicotine addiction.

The anger and irritability I experience are a stage in my recovery from the nicotine addiction. No magic cure will take them painlessly away. I must grow through experiencing these feelings and honestly dealing with them, at long last.

Today, I will bravely face
all emotions.

At the end of my life I will not be asked, "why
were you not Moses?" I will be asked "why were
you not Zusya?"

—RABBI ZUSYA

It is useful to stop and reflect on the growth I have gained since I quit
using nicotine. What a terrible pun. Yes, I have had some growth I
will want to drop. When it is the right time I will diet and return to
my best weight. I will not allow weight gain to sabotage my new freedom
from nicotine.

Getting on with the idea of reflecting on the progress since quitting:
Have I discovered any insights to enjoying life? Certainly I have found
physical benefits. I do not wake up with a groggy brain now, to name
just one. But how about the hope I now feel? I am no longer causing
constant damage to my body. The damage will be healed as I stay quit. I
also have relief from my worries about my addiction.

What if I have seriously harmed my body already? I could say, "fine,
there's no point in quitting, is there? I might as well keep on." One
Nicotine Anonymous member had already lost one lung when she joined
the Program. She explained that her new-found recovery was precious to
her, and she refused to lose it by going back to the nicotine addiction. I
need to recognize progress before I can place a value on it.

---

*Today, I will take a moment to congratulate myself and
reflect on my lessons learned. I enjoy real satisfaction for
the physical and personal progress I find.*

> Let us look at our own faults, and not at other
> people's. We ought not to insist on everyone
> following in our footsteps, nor to take upon
> ourselves to give instruction in spirituality when,
> perhaps, we do not even know what it is.
>
> —TERESA OF AVILA

Meetings bring many different people together with one common purpose: the desire to quit using nicotine. This is a selfish Program. I go to meetings to gain the benefits of the Program. I want to stay free of nicotine addiction for the rest of my life.

I may find that the meetings are not satisfying my needs. One member or a small group may seem to dominate, meeting after meeting. Is this good? Are these members sharing their experiences in quitting? Are they sharing knowledge of the Program? This may be to everyone's benefit. Instead of reacting, I can listen and learn.

Before I attempt to change another person, let me honestly look at my own actions at meetings. Do I dwell on the addiction as I talk, or do I focus on the tools of recovery that the Program offers? Do I put the spotlight on my struggles and difficulties with the addiction, or do I show how I have worked to overcome the addiction, the precious victories? Do I judge others for their education or money instead of listening for their growth and spiritual message?

Today, I will let our Traditions guide me
in handling the problems that arise
when any group of people gathers.

The Twelve Steps of Nicotine Anonymous

1. We admitted we were powerless over nicotine—that our lives had become unmanageable.

2. Came to believe that a Power greater than ourselves could restore us to sanity.

3. Made a decision to turn our will and our lives over to the care of God as we understood Him.

4. Made a searching and fearless moral inventory of ourselves.

5. Admitted to God, to ourselves, and to another human being the exact nature of our wrongs.

6. Were entirely ready to have God remove all these defects of character.

7. Humbly asked Him to remove our shortcomings.

8. Made a list of all persons we had harmed, and became willing to make amends to them all.

9. Made direct amends to such people wherever possible, except when to do so would injure them or others.

10. Continued to take personal inventory and when we were wrong promptly admitted it.

11. Sought through prayer and meditation to improve our conscious contact with God as we understood Him, praying only for knowledge of His will for us and the power to carry that out.

12. Having had a spiritual awakening as the result of these steps, we tried to carry this message to nicotine users and to practice these principles in all our affairs.

The Twelve Steps of Alcoholics Anonymous

1. We admitted we were powerless over alcohol—that our lives had become unmanageable. 2. Came to believe that a Power greater than ourselves could restore us to sanity. 3. Made a decision to turn our will and our lives over to the care of God as we understood Him. 4. Made a searching and fearless moral inventory of ourselves. 5. Admitted to God, to ourselves, and to another human being the exact nature of our wrongs. 6. Were entirely ready to have God remove all these defects of character. 7. Humbly asked Him to remove our shortcomings. 8. Made a list of all persons we had harmed, and became willing to make amends to them all. 9. Made direct amends to such people wherever possible, except when to do so would injure them or others. 10. Continued to take personal inventory and when we were wrong promptly admitted it. 11. Sought through prayer and meditation to improve our conscious contact with God as we understood Him, praying only for knowledge of His will for us and the power to carry that out. 12. Having had a spiritual awakening as the result of these steps, we tried to carry this message to alcoholics, and practice these principles in all our affairs.

The Twelve Traditions of Nicotine Anonymous

1. Our common welfare should come first; personal recovery depends upon Nicotine Anonymous unity.
2. For our group purpose there is but one ultimate authority—a loving God as He may express Himself in our group conscience. Our leaders are but trusted servants; they do not govern.
3. The only requirement for Nicotine Anonymous membership is a desire to stop using nicotine.
4. Each group should be autonomous except in matters affecting other groups or Nicotine Anonymous as a whole.
5. Each group has but one primary purpose—to carry its message to the nicotine addict who still suffers.
6. A Nicotine Anonymous group ought never endorse, finance or lend the Nicotine Anonymous name to any related facility or outside enterprise, lest problems of money, property and prestige divert us from our primary purpose.
7. Every Nicotine Anonymous group ought to be fully self-supporting, declining outside contributions.
8. Nicotine Anonymous should remain forever non-professional, but our service centers may employ special workers.
9. Nicotine Anonymous, as such, ought never be organized; but we may create service boards or committees directly responsible to those they serve.
10. Nicotine Anonymous has no opinion on outside issues; hence the Nicotine Anonymous name ought never be drawn into public controversy.
11. Our public relations policy is based on attraction rather than promotion; we need always maintain personal anonymity at the level of press, radio, television and films.
12. Anonymity is the spiritual foundation of all our Traditions, ever reminding us to place principles before personalities.

The Twelve Traditions reprinted and adapted with permission of Alcoholics Anonymous World Service. Inc. Permission to reprint and adapt the Twelve Traditions does not mean that AA is affiliated with this program. AA is program of recovery from alcoholism—use of the Twelve Traditions in connection with programs and activities which are patterned after AA. but which address other problems. does not imply otherwise.

The Twelve Traditions of A.A.
1. Our common welfare should come first: personal recovery depends upon A.A. unity. 2. For our group purpose there is but one ultimate authority—a loving God as He may express Himself in our group conscience. Our leaders are but trusted servants; they do not govern. 3. The only requirement for A.A. membership is a desire to stop drinking. 4. Each group should he autonomous except in matters affecting other groups or A.A. as a whole. 5. Each group has but one primary purpose—to carry its message to the alcoholic who still suffers. 6. An A.A. group ought never endorse. finance or lend the A.A. name to any related facility or outside enterprise lest problems of money, property and prestige divert us from our primary purpose. 7. Every A.A. group ought to he self-supporting, declining outside contributions. 8. Alcoholics Anonymous should remain forever non-professional but our service centers may employ special workers. 9. A.A.. as such. ought never he organized; but we may create service boards or committees directly responsible to those they serve. 10. Alcoholics Anonymous has no opinion on outside issues hence the A.A. name ought never he drawn into public controversy. 11. Our public relations policy is based on attraction rather than promotion; we need always maintain personal anonymity at the level of press, radio and films. 12. Anonymity is the spiritual foundation of all our traditions, ever reminding us to place principles before personalties.

Index